Department of Health and the Welsh (

GW00738342

Working Together
A guide to arrangements for inter-agency co-operation for the protection of children from abuse

London: HMSO

© *Crown copyright 1988*
First published 1988
Second impression 1991

ISBN 0 11 321154 6

Contents

WORKING TOGETHER

A GUIDE TO ARRANGEMENTS FOR INTER-AGENCY
CO-OPERATION FOR THE PROTECTION OF CHILDREN FROM
ABUSE

PART ONE: INTRODUCTION

1.1 Child abuse which requires local authority intervention falls within the provisions of section 1((2)(a) and (c)) of the Children and Young Persons Act 1969: 'his proper development is being avoidably prevented or neglected or his health is being avoidably impaired or neglected or he is being ill treated; or... he is exposed to moral danger'. The aim of this document is to provide a guide to all the agencies involved in working together to protect children from abuse. It is essentially concerned with how agencies can develop agreed joint policies and the arrangements necessary for making them effective, both in respect of individual cases and in respect of the monitoring and review of practice and related management issues. It draws on a wide ranging formal consultation exercise and informal discussions between the relevant Government Departments and professional staff involved at all levels in agencies about current arrangements and experience of them. It consolidates previous Departmental guidance on procedures and recommends developments aimed at making these more effective. It does not attempt to provide guidelines on the practice of individual professions in the recognition of child abuse or subsequent care or treatment but is concerned with inter-professional and inter-agency co-operation. It aims accordingly to provide a guide for all professional staff involved in the handling of child abuse cases. Hence some of the ground covered will be familiar to some and not to others. Strengthening the common basis of understanding is essential to the task involved and a particular objective of this guide.

1.2 It is important that all those likely to be professionally concerned with the protection of children whether or not employed by the local authority, have a clear understanding of the main points of child care law as it applies to the care and protection of children and its implications for the discharge of their respective responsibilities. They should be aware, in particular, that legislation places the primary responsibility for the care and protection of abused children and children at risk of abuse on local authorities; and that the nature of the responsibility a local authority carries in an individual case will

5

vary according to whether or not there has been court intervention and on the outcome of any proceedings.

1.3 Other agencies besides local authorities have statutory duties and or powers and all agencies have specific functions and professional objectives. In working together for the protection of children, however, they need to understand that they are not only carrying out their own agency's functions but are also making, individually and collectively, a vital contribution to advising and assisting the local authority in the discharge of its child protection and child care duties. **Therefore it is essential that wherever one agency becomes concerned that a child may be at risk they share their information with other agencies** as other agencies may have information which will clarify the situation. Inter-agency procedures should be brought into action at the earliest possible stage and in respect of every allegation. Such procedures should apply whether the child be living at home, with foster parents, in a residential home or in any other situation.

1.4 The following guidance summarises the responsibilities of the main agencies concerned and the groups of staff within them. Agencies should ensure that staff who are concerned with the protection of children from abuse understand the main points and relevance of the law, the role of other agencies and have access to legal advice.

1.5 This guidance should be read in the light of relevant guidance issued to individual agencies and professions. A list of such guidance can be found at Appendix 1.

PART TWO: LOCAL AUTHORITY SOCIAL SERVICES DEPARTMENTS

Statutory responsibilities

2.1 Social services, which include child care services, are provided by local authorities' social services departments acting under the general guidance of the Secretaries of State. Each local authority is required by the Local Authority Social Services Act 1970 to set up a Social Services Committee of elected members of the authority and to appoint a Director of Social Services.

2.2 Child care legislation which has as its main consideration the protection of children places upon the local authorities' social services departments statutory duties in relation to children. These statutory duties impose a responsibility to investigate reports of children at risk and to take the appropriate action to protect the child and to promote the welfare of the child. These child protection duties and responsibilities apply to all children in the community whether the child is living at home with parents or living with another carer, (who may be a local authority foster parent or residential worker). The primary responsibility of the social services department does not diminish the role of other agencies or the need for inter-agency co-operation in the planning and providing of services for a child or family. In particular the duty of the local and health authorities to co-operate in the exercise of their respective functions is set out in Section 22 of the National Health Service Act 1977.

2.3 Local authorities also have a statutory duty to act to prevent or remedy situations that could result in children coming into care and can act to help families whose circumstances may put a child at risk. Their action will be most effective when taken in collaboration with other agencies.

See Appendix 2 for details of legislation.

Investigation

Section 1–2 Child Care Act 1980
Section 2 Children and Young Persons Act 1969

2.4 It follows from the general duty of local authorities to promote the welfare of children that they investigate situations where it appears that there may be a need for social services support to promote the welfare of a child. Local authorities have a statutory duty to investigate where it is believed that a child is at risk and grounds for bringing care proceedings may exist. If their inquiries show that a child or a family do need support or services then the local authority must take the appropriate action, in accordance with its statutory duties and in collaboration with other agencies. Such action should take place whether the child be living at home, with foster parents, in a residential home or in any other situation.

Prevention

Section 1 Child Care Act 1980

2.5 Social services departments have a statutory duty to make available advice, guidance and assistance to promote the welfare of children by diminishing the need to receive children into care or bring them before a juvenile court. The need for such support may be identified either by families themselves, by involved agencies or others. Local authorities and voluntary organisations provide a variety of services to meet the needs of families for support and assistance in caring for children. They have discretionary powers to provide day care services, a discretionary power to grant aid voluntary groups and a duty to satisfy themselves as to the well being of privately fostered children. The Foster Children Act 1980 gives local authorities the duty to satisfy themselves as to the well-being of privately fostered children and to secure that such advice is given as to their care and maintenance as appears to be needed. Section 21 of the National Health Service Act 1977 empowers local authorities to provide services for the care of pre-school children. Day nurseries, play groups, childminding, family aides, family centres and other facilities which offer support and advice are used in preventive work with families.

Reception into care (voluntary care)

Section 2 Child Care Act 1980

2.6 Despite the provision of social work support and services the local authority may decide that it is necessary to receive a child into care. Such action by the local authority does not require court proceedings where parents request or willingly accept that a child should be received into the care of the local authority under section 2, or the other provisions of section 2 apply. In these cases parental rights and duties are not transferred to the local authority. The social workers involved with the child should assess the child's needs and prepare a plan to promote and safeguard the welfare of the child throughout its childhood. The welfare principle applies in all situations in which a child is in care, see section 18(1) Child Care Act 1980.

Care proceedings

Section 2 Children and Young Persons Act 1969

2.7 When supportive and preventive action has failed or is deemed inappropriate or insufficient to protect a child at risk a decision must be taken on whether or not to institute care proceedings. If it seems to a local authority following investigation that there are grounds for bringing care proceedings for any or all of the children in a household then the local authority has the duty to institute such proceedings. The police and the NSPCC also have powers, but not a duty, to bring care proceedings and in most cases proceedings are brought by the local authority.

Emergency situations

Section 40   Children and Young Persons Act 1933
Section 23   Children and Young Persons Act 1963
Section 28   Children and Young Persons Act 1969

2.8 Legislation does not enable social workers to enforce entry in pursuance of their investigative duties. When it is suspected that a child is being ill-treated or is in some other grave danger a place of safety order can be sought to secure the immediate removal of a child from home. Any person may apply to a magistrate for a 'place of safety order' but in practice most orders are obtained by local authority social services departments or place of safety action is taken by the police.

2.9 The order authorises the person named in it to detain the child in a place of safety for up to twenty eight days. A place of safety can be a relative's home, a hospital, a police station, a residential children's home or other suitable place. Twenty-eight days is the maximum period of time for which a place of safety order can be made; where police remove a child pursuant to Section 28(2) of the Children and Young Persons Act 1969 they can only keep the child for eight days. The order does not transfer parental rights and duties but the person to whom the order is granted is responsible for the child's safety and welfare during the currency of the order. This may entail arranging a medical examination, at which any need for medical treatment and follow-up will be assessed and arranged.

2.10 A place of safety order does not give the applicant the right to enter premises without the householder's consent in order to remove a child. When entry is likely to be, or is refused a police warrant can be obtained under section 40 of the Children and Young Persons Act 1933. Where speed is essential to protect a child and a warrant would take too long to obtain the police can enter premises without a warrant to save life or limb under Section 17(1)(e) of the Police and Criminal Evidence Act 1984.

2.11 The usual procedure after the granting of a place of safety order, if the child is not returned before the order expires, is for the local authority to apply for a care order or an interim care order. The parents and child can use the hearing at which the application for a care or an interim care order is considered to challenge the local authority's action by arguing that no order should be made. If no order is made, the child will go home.

Supervision orders

Sections 11–19 Children and Young Persons Act 1969

2.12 A court can dispose of care proceedings by making a supervision order which places a child under the supervision of the local authority in whose area the child lives, or a designated local authority which agrees to supervise the child, or a probation officer. While a supervision order remains in force it is the duty of the supervisor to advise, assist and befriend the supervised child.

2.13 A court can attach specific requirements to a supervision order; the requirement that a child be periodically medically examined may be attached to an order when a child is considered to be at risk of abuse. If such a requirement is not complied with Section 14A of the 1969 Act provides that a warrant to search for a child can be issued. Alternatively a supervisor can apply to the court for the discharge of the supervision order and the substitution of a full care order. It is not necessary in such cases to re-establish the primary ground as section 16(6) of the 1969 Act indicates that it is only necessary in these circumstances for the court to satisfy itself that the child needs care and control before making a care order.

The care order

Section 2 Children and Young Persons Act 1969

2.14 A care order under section 2 of the 1969 Act commits the child to the care of the local authority and gives the local authority the same powers and duties over the child as a parent would have if no order had been made, except that the local authority cannot change the child's religion, cannot agree to the child's adoption or to an application to free the child for adoption and cannot agree without consent of the Secretary of State to an emigration plan for the child.

2.15 The local authority retains parental rights and duties in respect of the child until the care order is revoked by a court or the child reaches the age of 18, irrespective of the child's actual placement; a child may be placed back at home with parents whilst remaining subject to the care order but parental rights and duties remain with the local authority.

Other proceedings

2.16 All agencies need to be aware that local authority social services departments may be given supervision or care of a child by a court following matrimonial or wardship proceedings. Equally it should be remembered that local authorities can instigate wardship proceedings where this appears to be appropriate.

Local authority responsibilities

Sections 10 and 18 Child Care Act 1980

2.17 The existence of a care order or supervision order in no way diminishes the need for inter-agency co-operation in planning and monitoring service provision. The arrangements must, however, be consistent with discharge by the local authority of its responsibility as the legal parent of the child and its other statutory duties to the child. In acting as a responsible parent for the child, the authority must at all times, wherever the child is placed, ensure that other agencies are fully informed of the care or supervision order; and that the welfare needs of the child are identified and (as far as possible) met. Where children are in care, the local authority's monitoring role and child protection responsibility is reinforced in relation to both the services it provides itself, and also those provided by other agencies. This is critical to the proper discharge of its duty to the child.

2.18 The staff of other agencies providing services to the child and family must recognise their responsibilities to see that the local authority in its parental role is kept fully and immediately informed of all matters relevant to the welfare of the child. **They must, in short, treat the local authority – as represented by the responsible officers of the authority – as they would the natural parents of the child.** Again this applies irrespective of the actual placement of the child.

PART THREE: HEALTH SERVICES

Health Authorities

3.1 Health authorities have been directed by the Secretary of State for Social Services in England and Secretary of State for Wales to promote a comprehensive health service, including such provision of facilities for the care of expectant and nursing mothers and young children as are considered are appropriate as part of the health service. The Regulations made under the National Health Services Act 1977 set out health authority functions while section 21 and Schedule 8 to that Act identify the functions proper to local authorities. Health authorities provide maternity services and community health services for children which include domiciliary health visiting and child health clinics. Section 22 of the 1977 Act requires that in exercising their respective functions health authorities and local authorities shall co-operate. Section 26(3) of the 1977 Act also places a duty on health authorities to provide, so far as is reasonable, necessary and practical, services to enable local authorities to fulfill their functions relating among other matters to social services. Each Health Authority should identify a doctor and senior nurse to co-ordinate the provision of advice to social services departments.

The role of the Midwife and Health Visitor

3.2 During pregnancy and birth and the early care of children, parents are, of necessity, in contact with the maternity and child health services, and this offers opportunities for the preparation and support of parents in the care of children. Both medical and nursing staff have a part to play, but the major role is for the midwife and health visitor working together. Encouraging parents to take a responsible attitude to the care of their children and to seek appropriate help and support may do much to prevent child abuse. Child abuse is less likely if there is an affectionate and positive relationship between parents and baby. The need to promote this, particularly when babies have had to spend some time in hospital after birth, was emphasised in the Third Report of the Maternity Services Advisory Committee which was published in 1985 and has already been commended to health authorities. In Wales guidance has been issued under W H C(86)69.

Monitoring a child's development

3.3 Health surveillance programmes for children organised by health authorities include encouraging parents to bring their children to child health clinics, where health visitors and doctors will be involved in monitoring the child's development; and domiciliary visits by health visitors, especially in cases where the child has not been brought to a clinic. Similarly school nurses and doctors may be involved in monitoring the child's development after he/she has started school. These and other community health staff are well placed to identify children who are being harmed or who may be at risk of harm.

3.4 Staff in hospital departments see children in the course of their normal duties and need to be alert to indications of child abuse. Abused children may attend hospital accident and emergency departments as a consequence of injuries inflicted on them. Staff there need to be particularly alert to the possibility of child abuse, and seek specialist advice and assistance (for example from a consultant paediatrician or consultant radiologist) in the assessment to determine whether there are signs of a history of abuse. Other health authority staff especially paediatricians and child psychiatrists have major contributions to make to the continuing care and support of children.

3.5 Local authorities and voluntary child care agencies need to work closely with health authorities (and local general medical and dental practitioners) to provide health surveillance and to meet the day to day health care needs of children in care. Recommendations for the development of policy and good practice were commended to health and local authorities in the report of the Social Services Inspectorate in their Inspection of Community Homes, published in February 1986. Complementary themes were explored in 'Nursing in the Community' the report of the Community Nursing Review undertaken in Wales, published in November 1987.

Family Practitioner Services

3.6 Family Practitioner Committees have an important facilitating role in relation to their contractors, particularly general medical practitioners. In collaboration with other agencies they should ensure that local arrangements, for example on the timing of case conferences, are such that the key contribution of GPs, can be brought to bear effectively. They should also contribute to the monitoring of these arrangements.

3.7 General medical practitioners have a vital role to play in the protection of children. As family doctors, working closely with health visitors, and other members of the primary health care team, they are in a position to identify family stress situations which point to a risk of child abuse, or to notice in the child at an early stage indications of abuse in one form or another. As more general practitioners become involved in child health surveillance programmes their role in preventing child abuse and in protecting children will increase. While practitioners have responsibilities to both parents and children the protection of the child must be paramount. It is essential that whenever a practitioner becomes suspicious that a child may be at risk of, or is the subject of abuse, that these concerns are discussed with colleagues experienced in working with child abuse cases. The concerns should then be shared with the statutory services responsible for child protection ie social services, the NSPCC or the police. Where the family doctor is convinced that abuse has occurred the processes of consultation and referral may need to take place very quickly. The practitioner's knowledge of the family will contribute to strategy discussions and to case conferences and any subsequent assessment and planning for the children within the multi-disciplinary group. See Parts Five and Six.

3.8 Others in the family practitioner services – dentists, opticians and pharmacists – should be aware of the need to recognise the signs of abuse, and contact social services departments, the NSPCC or the police if they are concerned about an individual child.

PART FOUR: OTHER STATUTORY AND VOLUNTARY AGENCIES

Local Education Authorities

4.1 Many Local Education Authorities have already acted to ensure that the need for the involvement of teachers and other staff in local multi-agency procedures is understood. Teachers and other school staff are particularly well placed to observe outward signs of abuse, changes in behaviour or failure to develop. Education welfare officers and educational psychologists also have important roles because of their concern for the welfare and development of children. All staff in the education service, including the youth service, must be aware of the need for social services, the N S P C C or the police to be alerted, according to locally established procedures, when an individual child is thought to be in need of protection.

4.2 There should be a generally understood procedure in each school for notifying cases of suspected or identified abuse. It is important that the headteacher or another senior member of staff should have designated responsibility for liaising with social services and other relevant agencies over such cases.

4.3 The relevant school should be promptly notified by the social services department of the inclusion of a child's name on the Child Protection Register. The details notified should include the care status of the child and where possible what information has been made known to the parents about any allegations or suspicions of abuse. Schools will wish to pay particular attention to the attendance and development of such children and to report any cause for further concern. The social services department should inform the school of any decision to remove the child from the Child Protection Register and of termination of a care order as well as any change in the status or the placement of the child.

4.4 In the longer term schools may have a role in preventing abuse through the teaching they offer. Courses in personal and social education can help young people develop more realistic attitudes towards the responsibilities of adult life including parenthood. Some schools teach children more directly about the risks of child abuse and the means of protecting themselves.

Some schools provide practical child care courses which may contribute towards better parenting.

The Police

4.5 The police are involved in cases of child abuse as a consequence of their general responsibility for the protection of life and limb, the prevention and investigation of crime and the submission of cases for criminal proceedings. In preparing cases for submission to the Crown Prosecution Service the police work to a standard of proof beyond reasonable doubt which is not the same as the balance of probabilities on which a juvenile court must be satisfied in care proceedings. Even in cases where the police are not considering a submission in respect of a prosecution they may be in possession of information that is highly relevant to any decision taken about a child who may need protection from abuse.

4.6 As indicated in Appendix 2, the police have an emergency power, not available to other agencies to detain a child in a place of safety without prior application to a court or justice. Where speed is essential to protect a child and a warrant would take too long to obtain they can act without it to enter premises in order to save life or limb, Section 17(1)(e) of the Police and Criminal Evidence Act 1984.

4.7 Although the police will wish to ensure that all appropriate steps are taken for the protection of the child, the primary responsibility for this will fall to the social services department. There are acknowledged difficulties for the police and social workers in the initial investigation of an allegation of child abuse and in the interests of children methods of joint working need to be established. A number of police forces have already established joint investigation arrangements with their local social services departments. See Parts Five and Six.

Probation Service

4.8 Probation officers may become involved in cases of child abuse as a result either of their responsibility for the supervision of offenders, including those convicted of offences against children, or of their responsibility to the court for the supervision of children following marital breakdown. They may be able to identify potential cases and bring in other agencies when, through their work, they become concerned about the safety of a child. Arrangements exist to ensure that when offenders convicted of offences against children are discharged from prison, probation services inform the local authority in the area in which the discharged prisoner plans to reside. This allows the social services department to make inquiries and take action if they believe there may be danger to children residing at the same address.

National Society for the Prevention of Cruelty to Children (NSPCC)

4.9 Uniquely amongst voluntary bodies the NSPCC has a power to bring care proceedings in its own right. The NSPCC is a charitable organisation whose Royal Charter places upon it 'the duty to ensure an appropriate and speedy response in all cases where children are alleged to be at risk of abuse or neglect in any form'. Social workers employed by the NSPCC have a central concern to identify and prevent cruelty to children. Increasingly the Society is creating, in co-operation with local authorities, child protection teams to provide specialist services in certain areas. Such collaboration is essential if the best use is to be made of the Society's expertise in child protection work. The NSPCC services the child protection registers on behalf of social services departments in twelve areas of the country. It also contributes to local and national training, particularly multi-disciplinary training.

Other Voluntary Organisations

4.10 A wide range of voluntary organisations provide services to help parents under stress. Authorities should be alert to the opportunities to promote voluntary effort in their area, and ensure that there is good liaison with voluntary organisations. Staff in these and other voluntary services concerned with children and families can also help by bringing children who are thought to be in need of protection to the attention of the statutory agencies. Voluntary organisations may have children in their care whom they have placed in foster or residential homes. The local authority is still the agency with statutory responsibility for child protection.

Armed Services

4.11 The life of a service family differs in many respects from that of a family in civilian life. Although in England and Wales it is local authorities which have the primary responsibility for the care and protection of children, it is essential for the local authorities and other agencies to note these differences and share information with the service authority when a service family becomes the subject of a child abuse investigation. Unlike civilian life, responsibility for the welfare of service families is invested in the employing service and specifically in the commanding officer. In addition, service authorities are responsible for the housing of the family, their welfare support and for the medical services for service personnel. They control the movement of the family in relation to service commitments; the frequency of such moves makes it imperative that service authorities are fully aware of any child who is deemed at risk. Arrangements differ for the main services and for American Forces' bases here and for United Kingdom bases abroad; these arrangements are summarised in Appendix 3.

The Community

4.12 The community as a whole has a responsibility for the well-being of children. This means that all citizens should remain alert to circumstances in which children may be harmed. Individuals can assist the statutory authorities by bringing cases to their attention. Relatives, friends, and neighbours of children are particularly well placed to do so, but they must know what to do if they are concerned. They must also be confident, because of the difficult and sensitive nature of the situation, that any information they provide will be treated in a confidential way and used only to protect the interest of the child. They should know too that early action on their part is often the best way of helping a family stay together as well as protecting the child.

4.13 The availability locally of self help groups, telephone help lines and other counselling services often provided by volunteers can do much to help parents help themselves or to seek help from others when it is needed. Victim support schemes which are being set up in many areas may be in a position to offer help to young people who have been abused.

4.14 Social services departments should ensure that they have effective arrangements to allow members of the public to refer to them concern about individual children. The size and complexities of social services departments can make it difficult for members of the public to know how to contact relevant personnel. There is evidence of frustration on the part of the public over this. Social services departments should publicise widely a telephone number which can be used by people concerned about a child. Sites for publicity could include public libraries, health clinics, community centres, family doctor's waiting rooms and other suitable local premises.

PART FIVE: WORKING TOGETHER IN INDIVIDUAL CASES

Introduction

5.1 Inter-disciplinary and inter-agency work is an essential process in the professional task of attempting to protect children from abuse. Local systems for inter-agency co-operation have been set up throughout the country in the past decade in response to Departmental guidance. The experience gained by professionals in working and training together, has succeeded in bringing about a greater mutual understanding of the roles of the various professions and agencies and a greater ability to combine their skills in the interest of abused children and their families.

5.2 Improvements in professional practice and inter-agency co-operation are still necessary and procedures still need to be further developed. Working arrangements need to involve all agencies and include the handling of cases of child sexual abuse. The thrust now must be to ensure that professionals in individual agencies work together on a multi-disciplinary basis. To achieve this end, agencies need to establish the individual training needs of their professionals and to ensure that they receive necessary training on a single discipline and multi-discipline basis.

Exchange of information

5.3 Arrangements for the protection of children from abuse, and in particular case conferences, can only be successful if the professional staff concerned do all they can to share and exchange relevant information, in particular with social services departments (or the NSPCC) and the police. Those in receipt of information obtained in this context to protect children must treat it as having been given in confidence. They should not disclose such information for any other purpose without consulting the person who provided it.

5.4 Ethical and statutory codes concerned with confidentiality and data protection are not intended to prevent the exchange of information between different professional staff who have a responsibility for ensuring the protection of children. The Annual Report 1987 of the General Medical Council gives unequivocal advice on this matter in cases of child abuse, including child sexual abuse:

'The Council's published guidance on professional confidence states that doctors may disclose confidential information to the police who are investigating a grave or very serious crime, provided always that they are prepared to justify their actions if called upon to do so. However, a specialist in child psychiatry recently drew to the Council's attention that its guidance does not specifically address the question of whether a doctor may properly initiate action in a case of this kind, as opposed to responding to a request. Both the British Medical Association and the medical defence societies have expressed the view that in such circumstances the interests of the child are paramount and that those interests may well override the general rule of professional confidence. On the recommendation of the Standards Committee, the Council in November 1987 expressed the view that, if a doctor has reason for believing that a child is being physically or sexually abused, not only is it permissible for the doctor to disclose information to a third party but it is a duty of the doctor to do so.'

5.5 The United Kingdom Central Council for Nursing, Midwifery and Health Visiting published in April 1987 A UKCC Advisory Paper on Confidentiality, this states:

'In all cases where the practitioner deliberately discloses or withholds information in what he/she believes is the public interest he/she must be able to justify the decision. These situations can be particularly stressful, especially where vulnerable groups are concerned, as disclosure may mean the involvement of a third party as in the case of children or the mentally handicapped. **Practitioners should always take the opportunity to discuss the matter fully with other practitioners** (not only or necessarily fellow nurses, midwives and health visitors), and if appropriate consult with a professional organisation before making a decision. There will often be ramifications and these are best explored before a final decision as to whether to withhold or disclose information is made.'

5.6 Staff in different agencies, and other practitioners, will maintain their own records of the case and such records should be subject to the arrangements for maintaining confidentiality within that particular agency. All agencies must establish procedures to safeguard information provided to them and to ensure timeous transfer of relevant records when a child and/or family moves to or from an area.

Stages of work in individual cases

5.7 If co-operation between agencies in providing protection to children is to be effective it must be underpinned by a shared understanding of the handling of individual cases. Although terminology may vary in different professions, they all go through a similar process of identifying a problem, studying it, deciding what to do and implementing those decisions. These stages can be identified in the following broad terms:

a. Recognition and Investigation;
b. Assessment and Planning;
c. Implementation and Review.

In using these terms it is not intended to imply that these stages are clearly divided in time as there will be some overlap. However, the sequence should enable professionals to see more clearly the focus of work at each stage and the purpose of the case conference in relation to it.

Recognition and investigation

5.8 The starting point of the child protection system in England and Wales is that any person who has knowledge or a suspicion that a child is being abused or is at risk of abuse has a duty to refer their concern to one or more of the agencies with statutory duties and/or powers to investigate and intervene. These are the 'investigating agencies', ie the social services department, the NSPCC and the police. Agency roles are outlined in Parts Two to Four of this guidance.

5.9 All professionals whose work is concerned with children and families should be alert to signs that a family is under stress and in need of help in the care and parenting of their children. They should know how to refer them to the statutory and voluntary agencies for help. They should also have a basic knowledge of how to recognise child abuse and make appropriate referrals to local investigating agencies. In cases where they suspect abuse but are not sure whether to make a referral, they should seek advice from senior staff or designated advisers in their own agency, a local multi-disciplinary advisory group or from the investigating agencies direct.

5.10 There is a need to investigate whenever a case is referred alleging abuse. All allegations should be regarded as serious, especially those made by close relatives, friends or neighbours, or by children or parents referring themselves for help, and investigated urgently. It is equally important that child abuse is recognised and investigated in cases already known to agencies but where the issue of child protection was not the reason for the initial referral or current involvement. It is essential that local authorities do not lose sight of the need to invoke child protection procedures when an allegation is made concerning abuse of a child in a local authority placement.

5.11 The initial steps for the investigating agencies must be to establish the relevant factual circumstances of the child and the possible sources of harm or danger. Child abuse cases involve both child care and law enforcement issues and what is discovered may be relevant to decisions which have to be taken by both social services or the NSPCC and the police. Close co-operation between these agencies from the outset is essential and local guidelines should be agreed between them on the investigation of individual cases. These should include strategy discussions with each other, relevant agencies and medical personnel, at an early stage in investigation. The purpose of these discussions is to ensure an early exchange of information and to clarify what action needs to be taken.

5.12 If there is reason to believe that the child is in immediate danger of harm, a decision must be taken urgently whether the child can remain at home, return home, or whether the child should be removed to a hospital or elsewhere, either on a voluntary basis or by obtaining a place of safety order. A place of safety order should only be sought for the minimum time necessary to ensure protection of the child. The position of any other children in the household must be considered at the same time. The dominant issue must be to ensure the safety of the child or children. Whenever possible these considerations should be brought to a multi-disciplinary case conference but in urgent cases action may need to be taken before the case conference.

5.13 The investigation of child abuse or risk of abuse **always requires social as well as medical assessment.** Co-operation with doctors is essential during the investigation to arrange for examination of the child and any treatment needed and to help in establishing whether or not on the balance of probabilities child abuse has occurred. Doctors need to record their findings and opinions contemporaneously for the purpose of contributing to future planning, including possible court action. Local procedures should provide for arrangements to avoid subjecting a child to repeated medical examinations solely for evidential purposes. Medical evidence which may be inconclusive when seen in isolation may help to provide a clear picture of abuse when seen in conjunction with other evidence. If the statutory agencies decide that compulsory intervention is needed, supporting medical evidence is clearly desirable but if not obtainable the other evidence may be sufficient in itself to show the degree of risk and protection required.

5.14 An inter-agency case conference should be convened by the social services department (or by the NSPCC in areas where this function is undertaken by the NSPCC in agreement with the social services department). The purpose of this is to try to ensure that all relevant information is pooled and that the case is handled on a multi-agency, multi-disciplinary basis co-ordinated by a child care agency with statutory powers.

5.15 The timing of the first inter-agency case conference will vary. The investigating agencies need to act with the speed appropriate to the circumstances of the case, co-ordinating their action with each other in accordance with locally agreed inter-agency procedures. In some cases, the first case conference will be held after the investigating agencies have held a strategy discussion, completed initial investigations and have taken urgent action to protect the child. In other cases, the first case conference will be held earlier in the process and may be involved in pooling information about suspected abuse and identifying ways in which it might be investigated. Whatever the timing, it is important that all invited to the case conference recognise the need for their attendance at the meeting and that participants understand the purpose for which the conference is being held. See paragraph 5.38.

5.16 The investigative stage is concluded when, following the sharing and discussion of all relevant information at an inter-agency case conference, the conference is able to reach a view on whether or not the child's name should be placed on the local child protection register. See paragraph 5.30.

5.17 The names of all children whose situations fit the register criteria should be registered and their cases will then be subject to co-ordinated inter-agency planning and review as described below. In those cases where the case conference view is that registration is not required it should not be overlooked that the child and family may still need a variety of services. Their requirements for services should be assessed and responded to by the relevant agencies as in other cases not involving child abuse procedures.

Assessment and planning

5.18 When an inter-agency case conference concludes that a child's name should be placed on the local child protection register, one of the child care agencies with statutory powers, ie the social services department or the NSPCC, should carry future child care responsibility for the case. The agency which is to carry this responsibility should designate at the case conference a member of its social work staff to act as 'key worker' for the purpose of co-ordinating inter-agency activity in the case.

5.19 It is not appropriate for anyone other than a social worker from either the social services department or the NSPCC to act as key worker. This does not mean that the key worker will necessarily need to be the person who has most face to face contact with the child and family or plays the most active role in any treatment or services provided. The key worker's role derives from the role of the lead agency, ie the agency with statutory child care powers which has the lead responsibility for the welfare and protection of the child in the individual case.

5.20 The primary task of the key worker will be to fulfill the statutory responsibilities of his or her agency which will include the development of a multi-agency, multi-disciplinary plan for the protection of the child. The key worker's secondary responsibility is to act as leading worker for the inter-agency work in the case. In this role he or she will provide a focus for communications between the professionals involved and will co-ordinate the inter-agency contributions to the assessment, planning and review of the case.

5.21 Any action to provide for protection, treatment and other services for the child and family must be based on an assessment of the child's and family's needs, including an assessment of the levels of risk to the child. Short-term plans may be based on an assessment made during or at the conclusion of the initial investigation. But longer-term plans require a comprehensive social, medical and developmental assessment. The key worker is responsible for ensuring that a more comprehensive assessment is prepared by his or her agency and for co-ordinating the contributions of other agencies to it. The key worker will also need to bear in mind the fact that other agencies may have statutory duties in relation to the family, for example probation officers supervising the offender or the child, if subject to a supervision order made to probation. It is the responsibility of the other agencies to ensure that they provide the key worker with the fullest co-operation in the preparation of a more comprehensive assessment. The completed assessment(s) need to be brought together at a case conference for discussion and the development of an inter-agency plan based on them. Discussion at a case conference, however, must not be used as a substitute for assessment work which should be carried out during the course of professional work with the child and family.

5.22 The key worker's agency, following consultation with the other agencies attending the case conference, should formulate a plan for the protection of the child and the provision of services to the child and family. The plan should clearly identify the contributions which individual agencies have stated they will make to it. Case conference conclusions will need to be framed in the light of agencies' statutory duties and all agencies will need to embody the case conference recommendations and their implications into their own work plans. This action plan should be recorded in the note of the case conference as the recommendations of the case conference to the constituent agencies and should include the arrangements for reviewing the plan.

Implementation and review

5.23 The responsibility to implement relevant parts of the plan and to communicate with the key worker and with each other, as needed, rests with individual agencies. The key worker is responsible for his or her agency's professional management of the case but, in addition, is responsible for providing a channel of communication between the involved agencies and for co-ordinating the inter-agency work as described above.

5.24 The inter-agency action plan should be formally reviewed at agreed intervals. The responsibility for ensuring this happens lies with the key worker's agency. The frequency and method of review should be suited to the needs of the case but a review should take place at least every six months. The review should be undertaken either by case conference or by written reports to the key worker in response to a request for such reports. A review should also be undertaken at significant points in the implementation of the plan; for example, when the viability of rehabilitation is being considered.

5.25 The main purpose of a review of the child protection plan is to review the working of the inter-agency plan designed to protect the child from abuse and ensure that his or her needs are being met and continuing safety afforded. The plan may also be concerned with reducing the risk of abuse for other children in future by, for example, reviewing the efficacy of treatment programmes for the child, the alleged abuser and others including family members. The review will, therefore, be concerned with looking at the problem areas which were identified in the assessment of the case, to see whether the plan's objectives are being achieved and, if not, making recommendations about alternative action. It will also be concerned with maintaining good inter-agency co-operation and the resolution of any difficulties which may arise.

24

5.26 When a child is in care, the local authority has a statutory duty to review the situation of the child at intervals of not more than six months. In conducting a statutory review the authority will, amongst other things, be concerned with any risk of abuse to the child and will, therefore, need to have available the reports of any inter-agency reviews undertaken between statutory reviews. Account should be taken of this need in the timing of reviews. When it is intended that a child protection review will be by case conference, consideration should be given to the feasibility of combining the review processes.

5.27 When a child protection review is conducted by reports to the key worker, it is essential that the reports are scrutinised, not only by the key worker and the key worker's supervisor, but also by at least one person who is not involved in working directly with the child and family or in direct supervision of that work. The person who would chair the review if it were to be held by case conference should scrutinise the reports, possibly assisted by others, for example, the key agency's child protection co-ordinator, specialist social work adviser or other specialist advisers to the key agency. If these scrutineers have concerns about the case, arising from the review reports, the key worker's agency should ensure that appropriate action is initiated which may include the convening of a review case conference. Similarly, any professional writing a report to the key worker for the purpose of the review may ask for a review by case conference, if in his or her professional judgement a face to face meeting is needed.

5.28 When the professionals who are working with the child and family decide that the risk to the child has been eliminated or reduced to an acceptable, minimal level the child's name should be removed from the child protection register. The decision to de-register should be taken as a result of a review which has sought the views on the de-registration of all those who have been working with the child and family, plus the views of any other professionals who were members of the initial case conference(s) in the investigative stage.

5.29 Removal of a child's name from the register should not lead to an automatic withdrawal or reduction in services. The risk of child abuse may have been eliminated or reduced but a variety of services may still be needed by the child and family, and in some cases the child will be in the care of the local authority either on a voluntary or compulsory basis.

Child protection registers

5.30 In each area covered by a social services department a central register must be maintained which lists all the children in the area who have been abused or who are considered to be at risk of abuse and who therefore are currently the subject of an inter-agency plan to protect them. The register should include children who are recognised to be at risk and who are placed in the local authority's area by other local authorities or agencies. As the information to be held on the register is concerned primarily with future protection of the child rather than past abuse, it is recommended that the register be renamed the child protection register. See Appendix 4.

5.31 The following categories of registration of abuse are not necessarily exhaustive nor are they mutually exclusive. The term 'child abuse' in this guide is intended to cover all these categories. Professional staff need to consider systematically whether all or some of these categories of abuse are present, as well as the degree to which they are present, in the situation faced by each child in the household. Children may be harmed by a parent, sibling or other relative, a carer (ie persons who while not parents have actual custody of a child, such as a foster parent, or a staff member in a residential home) an acquaintance or a stranger. The harm may be the result of a direct act or by a failure to act to provide proper care, or both:

Neglect: The persistent or severe neglect of a child (for example, by exposure to any kind of danger, including cold and starvation) which results in serious impairment of the child's health or development, including non-organic failure to thrive.

Physical abuse: physical injury to a child, including deliberate poisoning, where there is definite knowledge, or a reasonable suspicion, that the injury was inflicted or knowingly not prevented.

Sexual abuse: The involvement of dependent, developmentally immature children and adolescents in sexual activities they do not truly comprehend, to which they are unable to give informed consent, or that violate the social taboos of family roles.

Emotional abuse: The severe adverse effect on the behaviour and emotional development of a child caused by persistent or severe emotional ill-treatment or rejection. All abuse involves some emotional ill-treatment; – this category should be used where it is the main or sole form of abuse.

Grave concern: Children whose situations do not currently fit the above categories, but where social and medical assessments indicate that they are at significant risk of abuse. These could include situations where another child in the household has been harmed or the household contains a known abuser.

5.32 The entry of a child's name on the register should normally only occur following discussion at a case conference when abuse or potential abuse is confirmed and an inter-agency agreement is made to work co-operatively to protect the child. The exception is that when a registered child moves the child should be registered at once pending the first case conference in the new area. A child's name will normally only be removed from the register when it is agreed in a case conference that formal inter-agency working is no longer necessary to protect the child. Once a child's situation is identified as fitting one of the above categories the child's name and details should be entered on the register with a record of the plan for the child and the services to be provided. **The purpose of the register is to provide a record of all children in the area who are currently the subject of an inter-agency protection plan and to ensure that the plans are formally reviewed at least every six months.** The register will provide a central point of speedy inquiry for professional staff who are worried about a child and want to know whether the child is the subject of an inter-agency protection plan; and will provide information for managers.

5.33 It is recommended that the register is established and maintained by the social services departments or the NSPCC on its behalf. The register should be held separately from agency records, in conditions safeguarding confidentiality. It should be managed by an experienced social worker with knowledge and skills in child abuse work (the register 'custodian'). This social worker, or named deputy, should be available to provide advice to professional staff making inquiry of the register. Information about how to contact the custodian should be available to all the agencies concerned and kept up to date.

5.34 A record should be kept of any children not on the register about whom enquiries are made, and of the advice given. If the child's name is on the register when an enquiry is made the name of the key worker should be given to the enquirer. If a child's name is not on the register when an enquiry is made but there is another child on the register at the same address the custodian should see that this is followed up.

5.35 When a registered child moves, the custodian should alert by telephone the custodian in the area to which the child has moved, confirmation of the information should be made in writing. The new area custodian should ensure that the child is registered in the new area at once pending the holding of a case conference there. A child's name will normally only be removed from the register when it is agreed in a case conference that formal inter-agency working is no longer necessary to protect the child.

5.36 Most cases of child abuse will involve children resident in the local area but experience has shown that some families in which children are harmed move home frequently. There is a real danger that in this way children can drop through the safety net and only reappear when serious harm has occurred. The custodian of the register should have, as a specific responsibility, the setting in hand of immediate action to try to trace families on the register who go missing. The custodian should also have responsibility for notifying liaison officers in other agencies of the need to transfer records when a family/child moves to another area.

5.37 The DHSS holds a list of custodians of child protection registers for England and Welsh Office will be maintaining a list for Wales. Whenever a change is made this should be notified to Community Services Division at Alexander Fleming House or HSSPI Division at Welsh Office as appropriate so that the list can be kept up to date.

Case conferences

5.38 Case conferences are an essential feature of inter-agency co-operation and the need for holding a conference should always be identified at an early stage. Case conferences should have a clear purpose, they are not an end in themselves. If they are too large, wrongly timed, have no clear purpose, involve the wrong people or are poorly conducted they may not only fail to facilitate good practice but may also bring inter-agency working into disrepute and undermine good practice.

5.39 Case conferences provide a forum for the exchange of information between professionals involved with the child and family and allow for inter-agency, multi-disciplinary discussion of allegations or suspicions of abuse; the outcome of investigation; assessments for planning; an action plan for protecting the child and helping the family; and reviews of the plan. The Chairman of the conference must be able to call upon the attendance of a lawyer from the local authority's legal section to assist in the evaluation of evidence indicative of care proceedings. The result of the discussions are recommendations to individual agencies for action. While the decision to implement the recommendations must rest with the individual agency concerned, any deviation from them should not be made, except in an emergency, without informing other agencies through the key worker.

5.40 For reasons of both efficiency and confidentiality the number of people involved in a case conference should be limited to those with a need to know or those who have a contribution to make to the task involved. A case conference may be larger in the early stages of work, when a number of agencies may be contributing to an investigation or to an assessment for planning. Once a long-term plan has been formulated, however, a small group including the key worker, should be identified as the core group who agree to work together to implement and review the plan.

5.41 A case conference is an inter-professional meeting but on occasion it may wish to invite a non-professional who is working with the child or family, for example, foster parents or volunteer workers. In this event, the key worker or the professional most closely involved with the non-professional should undertake to brief him or her beforehand about the purpose of the conference, the duty of confidentiality and the primacy of the child's interests over that of the parents if a conflict of interest arises.

5.42 Case conferences should be convened by the social services department or the NSPCC on its behalf but other agencies should be able to request one in the expectation that the request will not be refused without good reason.

5.43 Those who are invited to a case conference but who are unable to attend should ensure that their contribution is made through a written note to the Chairman. Particular attention should be paid to arranging case conferences so that those with inflexible commitments, for example single handed general medical practitioners or teachers, can attend.

5.44 Case conferences should only be chaired by a senior staff member of the social services department or the NSPCC with the appropriate skill and experience to chair conferences and who does not have direct involvement in the case. The main tasks of the Chairman are to ensure that:

a. conferences maintain a focus on the child as the primary client whose interests must transcend those of the parent where there is any conflict;
b. the purpose of the particular conference is made clear;
c. the people present are the ones required for the fulfilment of that purpose;
d. all those present contribute and full consideration is given to their contribution;
e. the key worker and the core group are identified;
f. a plan, based on assessment and clearly understood by all concerned, is developed and agreed, for recommendation to the agencies concerned, and any reservations or dissenting views recorded;
g. arrangements for review of the plan and the date of the first review are agreed;
h. agreement is reached with the key worker about how parents or carers will be informed of the plan for inter-agency co-operation and the purpose of the child protection register; and
i. a written note of the case conference which records those participating, absentees and the recommendations, is made and its circulation list agreed.

Not all of these tasks will be relevant to every case conference. The person chairing the meeting should not take the note of the meeting but should be responsible for checking its accuracy.

Involvement of children and parents

5.45 It is important that parents and/or carers be informed about the basis of an investigation or intervention. Agencies need to be aware that the European Court of Human Rights, in finding the United Kingdom Government to be in breach of Articles six and eight of the European Convention of Human Rights in recent child care cases, cited failure to involve the parents in decision making as a factor in their judgements. Parents need to know the reasons for professional concern, the statutory powers, duties and roles of agencies involved, their own legal rights and the changes in the family's situation which the agencies consider necessary or desirable in the interests of the child. Openness and honesty and the ability of professional staff to use authority appropriately are an essential basis on which to build a foundation of understanding between parents and professionals. Parents should be informed or consulted at every stage of investigation. Their views should be sought on the issues to be raised prior to a case conference to afford them the opportunity to seek advice and prepare their representations. They should be invited where practicable to attend part, or if appropriate the whole, of case conferences unless in the view of the Chairman of the conference their presence will preclude a full and proper consideration of the child's interests. Parents should be informed of the outcome of a case conference as soon as is practicable and this information should be confirmed in writing.

5.46 When a child is in the care of the local authority that authority has a specific duty to promote the welfare of the child and, in relation to any decisions taken, to ascertain as far as is practicable his or her wishes and feelings and give due consideration to them, having regard to his or her age and understanding. This principle should be extended to include children who are the subject of a case conference but are not in the care of the local authority. Whenever children are old enough to express their wishes and feelings and to participate in the process of assessment, planning and review, the case conference should be provided with a clear and up to date account of their views by the professionals who are working with them. The case conference should, therefore expect the key worker to be able to inform them about the views of a child. Equally the child should be kept informed of the progress of the inter-agency work by the professional working with him or her.

5.47 When an agreement has been reached in a case conference to place the child's name on the child protection register and to formalise inter-agency co-operation, the parents or carers and where it is appropriate, the child should be informed of this agreement and its purpose. The function of case conferences and the child protection register in facilitating the inter-agency work should be explained at the same time. Parents should be advised of the procedure for removal of the child's name and when registration might end and that they will be informed if and when this happens.

5.48 It is good practice in all professions to confirm important information to parents in writing. Written confirmation of the inter-agency action plan should, with the agreement of the agencies concerned, be provided for parents by the key worker. This could set out the reasons for the plan, the services to be provided for the family and the parents and agencies' expectations of each other. It is important, however, that parents are not misled as to where the responsibility for decision-making lies. For example, the decision to initiate care proceedings lies with the agencies with statutory powers. Parents and their legal advisers who wish to discuss or challenge a decision of this kind need to take it up with the agency concerned; it is not a matter for the case conference which is a consultative, advisory body not a body with executive powers. Similarly, parents who have a complaint about a particular agency's service should take it up with the agency concerned. All agencies should ensure that they have clear procedures which will enable parents to pursue complaints. Agencies should ensure that all those involved in a case are provided with information about these procedures.

5.49 Parents whose care of their children becomes a matter for professional concern are bound to have a mixture of strong emotional reactions. One of the tasks of professionals is to acknowledge and work with such reactions without becoming defensive about the proper exercise of their professional responsibility. It is in the interest of all children and all parents that professionals should be alert to the possible need for intervention to protect children. On occasion, however, it will be found after investigation that allegations or suspicions are not substantiated. In these cases it is essential that this is made clear to parents and that any distress or inconvenience to them is acknowledged. In some cases supportive counselling will be needed as a follow up and an offer of counselling should always be considered.

Supervision

5.50 Professional staff dealing with child abuse cases must receive regular supervision. The supervisor's first task is to ensure that the practitioner is familiar not only with any internal practice and procedural guidelines but also with the legal framework relevant to child abuse work and with the local handbook of inter-agency procedures. The supervisor needs to ensure, through supervision, good management and relevant staff development, that the practitioner maintains a focus on the child as primary client and co-operates appropriately with other agencies, so that the case is handled on a multi-agency, multi-disciplinary basis.

Expert advice

5.51 For many staff involvement in child abuse cases are infrequent and access to expert advice will be needed. Some social services departments and other agencies have already designated individuals who can offer their staff expert advice. It is recommended that each agency concerned with child abuse should identify a suitably qualified and experienced officer in their own organisation to carry out this role for its staff.

5.52 Medical, psychiatric and nursing advice to social service departments is particularly important. Each health authority should identify a doctor and senior nurse to provide or arrange the provision of such advice on a regular basis. The doctor should provide liaison between all the medical services provided by the health authority, including both hospital and community services, and should establish links with the Family Practitioner Committee who would involve individual general practitioners and the local medical committee. The doctor and nurse identified should not necessarily be expected to attend every case conference but should be informed about every case and be readily accessible to provide expert advice. These arrangements should be co-ordinated with the procedures for the handling of complex cases involving sexual abuse set out in Part Six.

Inter-agency liaison

5.53 Officers identified to provide expert advice should also be given responsibilities for co-ordinating child abuse matters in the agency as a whole; for example to act as a liaison point for contact and co-ordination with other agencies, to promote good policy and practice developments within the agency, and advise on associated training needs. Identification of officers with experience to act as central points of advice and contact between and within agencies will do much to facilitate inter-agency co-operation.

5.54 Within social services departments, the social worker identified to provide expert advice should normally also be responsible for the management of the child protection register. Within Education Departments the official identified will normally act as the central point of contact, complementing the arrangements for liaison officers in each school. Similar arrangements should also be set up in other services. These arrangements must include the designation of an officer to be responsible for the transfer of records when a child and/or family moves to or from the area.

PART SIX: SEXUAL ABUSE CASES

Introduction

6.1 Sexual abuse of children, like other forms of abuse, has always existed. In the past few years professional staff have realised that its incidence is greater than previously assumed. The number of cases being identified is increasing and may continue to increase as professional staff become better able to recognise sexual abuse and as the public, including victims and perpetrators themselves, become more willing to report it or to seek help. Finding ways of responding effectively in individual cases poses a major challenge for all the professional staff involved. The present level of knowledge and skills may be compared to the level of knowledge and skills available on physical abuse about fifteen years ago. The experience gained in developing procedures for inter-agency co-operation and joint working by agencies on other forms of abuse will be helpful in developing similar procedures for co-operation on sexual abuse but will not be sufficient. Sexual abuse has features which require separate consideration in order to see how existing inter-agency procedures can be adapted to include it.

Handling of individual cases

6.2 Cases of child sexual abuse should be brought into the system of inter-agency co-operation described in this guide. The three stages of work described in Part Five apply equally to these cases. However, the handling of cases of child sexual abuse is usually complex and is a relatively new experience for many staff. It will take time to develop the necessary knowledge and skills.

6.3 Particular problems that need to be considered in the investigative stage are:

a. *Early detection:* Agency staff and independent practitioners need to be alert to behavioural factors indicating possible sexual abuse, as physical indications are not always present. When a suspicion of sexual abuse arises the exchange of information with other agencies will help to clarify the situation. Any allegation received by one of the investigating agencies should be communicated immediately to the others in accordance with the local multi-agency procedures so that strategy discussions can take place on how the investigation will be conducted. See paragraph 6.11.

b. *Evidence:* A particularly high level of co-operation between social services departments or the NSPCC and police and doctors is essential during the investigation because of the likely nature of the evidence. It is essential that no agency relies on any one criterion in isolation. As with other forms of child abuse discussion between agencies of all relevant factors is necessary to identify the cause of the child's condition on the balance of probabilities before deciding the appropriate action.

c. *Support and protection for the child:* Services must be available immediately to provide support and protection for the child if abuse is alleged. It is recognised that sexual abuse does not necessarily call for an immediate emergency response or removal of a child from home. However, care away from the family must be provided if there is reason to believe that a child may be subject to assault or intimidation. It may be appropriate for arrangements to be made with the carer or parents so that the child may remain at home. If the child needs care away from home it will be for the social services department to decide the type of placement and to make arrangements.

d. *Support for parents:* Services must be available to provide support and counselling to parents and family. It may be appropriate to allocate a separate social worker to the parents to provide information and advice and to discuss access arrangements. The principles set out in the 'Code of Practice – Access to Children in Care' should be applied in every case.

6.4 A child's statement about an allegation of abuse, whether in confirmation or denial, should always be taken seriously. A child's testimony should not be viewed as inherently less reliable than that of an adult. However, professionals need to be aware that a false allegation may be a sign of a disturbed family environment and an indication that the child may need help.

6.5 Lord Justice Butler-Sloss's report on Cleveland states:

'There is a danger that in looking to the welfare of the children believed to be the victims of sexual abuse the children themselves may be overlooked. The child is a person and not an object of concern.'

The child's welfare must be the overriding concern of professional staff who become involved in the case. The gathering of evidence of abuse must not become an additional source of abuse of the child, in either the short or long term. If the abuse has occurred within the previous forty eight hours the investigation may need to include the collection of forensic evidence by a suitably qualified doctor. The child should not be subjected to repeated medical examinations but referred initially to a suitably experienced doctor who is sensitive to the needs of children and issues involved, and who is experienced at giving medical evidence in court. This doctor could be a paediatrician, police surgeon, or other doctor who has this special expertise. Similarly police, social workers and doctors should not subject the child to unnecessary repeated interviewing. Medical examinations should be conducted in an appropriate clinical setting, which could be at the local hospital or in a doctor's surgery. Local procedures should include agreed arrangements for the carrying out of these examinations by nominated practitioners in designated settings. Further guidance on this and other medical aspects for medical practitioners by the Standing Medical Advisory Committee is being issued at the same time as this document.

6.6 The investigation of sexual abuse requires highly co-ordinated work by the police, social workers and doctors, who will be meeting informally to plan their work. In cases when allegations or suspicions cannot be immediately substantiated the investigating agency should hold discussions with other professionals as necessary to decide on the need for further investigation or to devise a strategy for pursuing the case. See paragraph 6.11 et seq. In other cases where there is an allegation or evidence of abuse the investigating agencies should proceed with the investigation and hold a case conference with all agencies and relevant professionals as soon as possible.

6.7 In cases of child abuse, including child sexual abuse, social services departments will give first and highest priority to protecting the child. However, they also have responsibilities in relation to the child's parents and other family members or carers. Social services departments have a particular responsibility to consider whether the objective of keeping the family together is in the child's best interests and, if not, to consider what alternative arrangements are to be made. The social services department will need to assess with the greatest care whether to deploy one or more social workers, and whether one social worker can adequately serve the interests of the child, the alleged abuser and other family members. They should, therefore, have regard to the need for practice guidance and supervision to assist the staff involved to acquire new skills and make the best use of all available resources within the context of the social services department's overall strategy for child care matters.

6.8 Where the abuse is due to distorted family relationships, for example cases of incest, assessment of the child and family's need for treatment must necessarily include consideration of whether appropriate resources are available locally. Where they are available, they can only be effective if provided within the context dictated by the law: the criminal law to which the abuser may be subject and the child care law which provides for the protection of children. Developing ways of providing treatment and rehabilitative services within the legal framework is a major task for inter-agency co-operation. It may be that a treatment and management plan for a known abuser and his family can be achieved by co-operation between all the relevant agencies thus avoiding a total family break-up (for example a father being required to live away from home, but accessible to and supporting the family during therapy). There are competing public interests in the handling of criminal offences and child protection. It may be possible for a case to be handled so that the interests of the child prevail over the public interest in dealing with an abuser and the prosecution not proceeded with but this will not inevitably be the case. Social services departments should ensure that the Police and the Crown Prosecution Service are aware of the child's best interests when considering a submission of a case for prosecution.

Specialist advice and guidance

6.9 Responding to child sexual abuse is a new area of work for many professional staff. In order to ensure that cases are handled with as much knowledge and skill as possible, the investigating agencies and the health authorities should try to ensure as far as is practicable that these cases are handled only by staff who have had preparation and training for the tasks involved and access to advice from experienced personnel.

6.10 Advice should be made available within each agency from members of staff who have gained expertise through training and experience. In addition to such internal advice, agencies should consider identifying a multi-disciplinary group of experienced professionals within each local authority area who could be contacted for advice and who could contribute to multi-disciplinary training.

Specialist assessment teams (SAT)

6.11 Where there is a suspicion of sexual abuse because of minor behavioural manifestations or inconclusive physical findings but where there has been no allegation or complaint of abuse by the child or a third party, there is a particular need for multi-disciplinary assessment using the best skills available in the area, in order to determine whether there is any cause for concern which would require further investigation or other action. Agencies are commended to consider carefully the conclusions and recommendations of the Report of the Inquiry on Child Abuse in Cleveland 1987 where Lord Justice Butler-Sloss recommends that the need for such an assessment will best be met by a SAT of social worker, doctor and police officer who would jointly undertake an initial assessment and advise on the need for further action, if any.

6.12 Lord Justice Butler-Sloss envisages that the team would be drawn from three local lists of suitably qualified and experienced professionals identified by the local authority, the health authority and the police respectively. The team would not normally carry any responsibilities for the case beyond what was involved in undertaking the initial assessment. Further details of how such a team could work are set out in the Report.

6.13 Some areas may decide that they are already providing a specialist multi-disciplinary assessment facility, equivalent to that which a SAT would provide, by virtue of having one or more specialist units for child abuse work involving collaboration between social workers, designated police officers and medical practitioners who are specialists in the field. Other areas will wish to explore the concept of the SAT. As with any other inter-agency arrangement, it would need to be carefully negotiated and embodied in written procedures agreed by the relevant agencies under the auspices of the Area Child Protection Committee, see Part Seven.

Supervision and training

6.14 Social workers, probation officers, doctors and others engaged in the long-term treatment of disturbed relationships in sexually abusing families need regular supervision and support. Work with these families makes considerable emotional demands and there is a tendency to over identify with an individual in the family and to be drawn into the collusive behaviour patterns within it. Arrangements to provide for both professional supervision and personal support for fieldworkers should exist in all agencies.

6.15 The professional supervision will identify individual training needs. Staff involved in investigating sexual abuse need training in the task, part of which should be on a multi-disciplinary basis involving police, social workers, health visitors, doctors and local authority lawyers. Training on the recognition of sexual abuse should be part of the training all relevant staff receive on child abuse generally. Social services departments should develop appropriate training strategies for their staff, to relate resources and planning to service objectives. These strategies should be subject to regular review and evaluation. They should also encompass initiatives for joint training as described in Part Eight.

Prevention

6.16 Attention needs also to be given to ways of preventing child sexual abuse. One means of prevention is to encourage earlier recognition and referral of families under stress and cases of suspected abuse. Training materials are and will become available which will provide a basis on which to build awareness and recognition skills of those professionals working with children and their families. The availability locally of services to provide effective intervention and treatment will encourage referrals by professional staff. Better information systems which facilitate the linking of information held within agencies will increase their effective response to reports received and should assist in better recognition of potential abuse situations.

6.17 Voluntary organisations and volunteer and self-help groups who offer informal counselling through drop-in centres, telephone help lines etc may facilitate earlier referrals from the public or self-referrals. However, the preventive measure with the greatest potential may be to enable children to protect themselves. The primary responsibility for this lies with parents but schools have made tentative steps in this field, within the broad context of health and safety education. More experience is needed to allow the efficacy and practicability of such programmes to be judged.

PART SEVEN: JOINT POLICIES AND PROCEDURES

Introduction

7.1 In every area there is a need for a close working relationship between social service departments, the police force, medical practitioners, community health workers and others who share a common aim to protect the child at risk. Co-operation at the individual case level needs to be supported by joint agency and management policies for child abuse, consistent with their policies and plans for related service provision. There needs to be a recognised joint forum for developing, monitoring and reviewing child abuse policies. Much of the progress in child abuse work in recent years can be attributed to the Area Review Committees (ARCs).

7.2 To be fully effective a joint forum needs to have a clearly recognised relationship to the responsible agencies. The pattern of ARCs has developed in a number of ways to reflect local boundaries and situations. Generally, one ARC has covered one local authority and all the district health authorities or parts of them within that local authority boundary.

7.3 The following paragraphs, drawing on the experience of ARCs to date and related developments, redesignate ARCs as Area Child Protection Committees (ACPCs) and make recommendations about accountability, organisation, funding, management information and reporting systems to assist ACPCs' effective operation and improve their accountability.

Accountability

7.4 ACPCs are accountable to the agencies which make up their membership. These agencies are jointly responsible for ACPC actions.

Representation

7.5 All agencies should recognise the importance of securing effective co-operation by appointing senior officers to the ACPC. Their appointees should have sufficient authority to allow them to speak on their agencies' behalf and to make decisions to an agreed level without referral to the appointee's agency. The level of decision making delegated to appointees needs to be considerable to enable ACPCs to operate effectively. Apart from senior officer representatives of health and social services, ACPC members will be senior officers from all the main authorities and agencies in the area which are involved in the prevention and management of child abuse. Detailed recommendations on the membership of ACPCs are provided in Appendix Five.

Chairmanship and secretariat

7.6 The responsibility for the provision of the Chairman and the secretariat and support services for the Committee should rest with the social services department. The Chairman should normally be an officer of the social services department of at least Assistant Director status and should preferably possess knowledge and experience of child protection work in addition to chairing skills. However, there may be situations where the social services department, with the agreement of the other Committee members, arranges for the Chairmanship to be undertaken on its behalf by a senior officer of one of the other agencies or by an independent person with the requisite knowledge, experience and chairing skills. In such a case, the Vice Chairman of the ACPC should be a senior officer of the social services department. The Director of the Social Services Department should ensure that his officers take the lead in monitoring implementation of the local procedures and the efficacy of arrangements and in making legal advice available to the ACPC.

Responsibilities of the ACPC

7.7 The ACPC should work to written, agreed, terms of reference which set out the remit of the ACPC and the level of decision which may be agreed by agencies' representatives without referral back to individual member agencies.

7.8 Each agency should accept that it is responsible for monitoring not only the performance of its own representative but also that of the ACPC. Each agency must have procedures for considering reports from its ACPC representative to identify any action necessary within the agency or the ACPC. Decisions which have implications for policy, planning and the allocation of resources need to be reported on and discussed at appropriate levels within agencies and made known to parent authorities (for example to the Joint Consultative Committees of Health and Local Authorities (JCC)) where appropriate.

7.9 Each ACPC should establish a programme of work to develop and keep under review local joint policies and procedures. The main areas of activity will be:

a. to establish, maintain and review local inter-agency guidelines on procedures to be followed in individual cases;
b. to review significant issues arising from the handling of cases and reports from inquiries;
c. to review arrangements to provide expert advice and inter-agency liaison;
d. to review progress on work to prevent child abuse;
e. to review work related to inter-agency training (see Part Eight).

Working groups

7.10 It is recommended that the ACPC establish working groups, which should include experienced field staff, to advise it and undertake detailed work on specific tasks. It may sometimes be appropriate to co-opt professionals with specialist knowledge to the groups. It is important for the ACPC to establish links with other organisations who may be able to help its work, examples are listed in Appendix Five.

Joint financing and expenses

7.11 It will be the duty of the agencies represented on an ACPC to reach agreements for funding the ACPC. Agencies should allocate funds to the ACPC in accordance with agreed arrangements at the beginning of each financial year so that the ACPC has an annual budget. A member of the ACPC should be appointed, with the support of his/her agency, to act as the officer responsible for funding. The provision of resources to support the secretariat should be established and joint financing by health and social services may be used for this purpose. When training is arranged on a multi-agency basis costs should be allocated accordingly.

7.12 The ACPC will need to reach agreement as to the expenses that may be incurred by the Committee and its working groups and to make such arrangements as may be agreed between them for the payment of such expenses. It is recommended that each agency represented on an ACPC should defray the expenses of its representatives.

Management

7.13 ARCs have already produced local procedural handbooks and these show a wide variety in both content and approach. They should be concerned mainly with inter-agency procedures, rather than detailed professional practice. The ACPCs should review and, where necessary revise these handbooks so that they represent a comprehensive and up-to-date statement of local policy. In the light of a study it made of existing handbooks the DHSS recommends a standard approach; a basic content and format is recommended in Appendix 6. Local procedural handbooks should be accessible in all agencies to all members of staff, and to independent practitioners in direct contact with children and families.

Information systems

7.14 Constituent agencies should make available to the ACPC, on a regular basis, management information to illustrate the level of activity on child abuse work, type and trends. The aim should be to produce this information quarterly. It should not include identifying details of individuals. The suggested content is outlined at Appendix 7.

7.15 Building on this information, each ACPC should review annually the work done to protect children from harm in their area and plan for the year ahead. These reviews and plans should take account of reports on the activity of any working groups. A report of the review and forward plan should be made by the ACPC to the head of each agency to underline that the accountability for the work of the ACPC rests with its constituent members. A recommended outline format for this report is at Appendix Eight. Extracts from the report could form the basis of local publicity to inform and involve the community at large in the work to protect children. A copy of the report should be sent to the DHSS Social Services Inspectorate in Regions and to JCCs for information. In Wales a copy of the report should be sent to the SWS Division of the Welsh Office and to local JCCs.

PART EIGHT: JOINT TRAINING

Introduction

8.1 Effective child protection depends not only on reliable and accepted systems of co-operation, but also on the skills of professional staff. Professional skills are achieved during basic qualifying training; during induction processes; through in-service specialist training and external post-qualifying courses. Basic qualifying training lies outside the remit of local agencies and is not addressed here. The following paragraphs recommend steps that agencies can take collectively to improve skills of the staff in handling cases of child abuse and in working on a multi-agency basis. Joint training must complement the action of individual agencies to promote the training and development of their own staff.

Professional staff

8.2 It is recommended that agencies should establish joint annual training programmes on child abuse issues for all professional groups in direct contact with children. These programmes should encompass the staff in all agencies to ensure a common understanding and thus foster good working relationships. The senior social worker providing expert advice to the local authority should play a central role in the development and monitoring of the arrangements for such training under the auspices of the ACPC. The key task will be to ensure that these training opportunities should be available and made known to staff in all the relevant agencies.

8.3 The level and type of training to be provided will depend upon the degree of involvement that the staff of particular agencies have in child abuse work. All relevant staff should be trained in the recognition of signs of potential abuse and what immediate action to take. Specialist training is more relevant to staff of social services departments, the NSPCC, the health service and the police who will be involved in the investigation of cases and subsequent intervention.

8.4 Child abuse training in the induction process of newly appointed staff has two purposes:

a. to provide or reinforce awareness among staff to signs of harm to children; and
b. to explain local policies and procedures.

Because of the large number of staff within the agencies involved, and for some, an infrequent involvement in the handling of child abuse cases, there is value in regular repeat training to reinforce these two essential elements.

8.5 Specialist in-service training should be directed primarily to those involved in the investigation of abuse and provision of protective services. It should reflect the need for knowledge and skill within the context related to child care law, the concept of child protection and the assessment of danger, and alternative forms of intervention. The central role of social services in child abuse work emphasises the need for this training for social workers; and the need in providing training should therefore be taken by the social services department. Arrangements should also be made to provide refresher courses to enable staff to keep their knowledge up to date. Part Six has indicated the current need to develop knowledge and skill in the handling of cases of child sexual abuse.

8.6 There are a limited number of post-qualifying courses in child care that have been approved by the Central Council for the Education and Training in Social Work. Where possible and appropriate, staff should be seconded to these. The DHSS central training initiative launched in October 1986 recognises the importance of training for managers and practitioners involved in child abuse work. The first stage of the initiative provides a training facility at the Department of Psychological Medicine at the Hospital for Sick Children at Great Ormond Street and a training advisory resource based at the National Children's Bureau under the aegis of the Training Advisory Group on the Sexual Abuse of Children. There are four projects in the second stage. The first involves the Open University in a two-year project to produce an introductory course on the problems of recognition and referral in cases of child abuse for professionals and others. The second is for a video and training pack on child sexual abuse for medical practitioners under the auspices of the Royal Society of Medicine. The other two projects cover inter-disciplinary working. Nottingham University are developing training materials on the inter-agency aspects of case conferences and the NSPCC is developing training for social workers and health visitors who need to provide expert advice to colleagues in their own agencies. Complementary initiatives are in hand for Wales.

8.7 Training is not a luxury, it is essential if manpower is to be used effectively. It is hoped that agencies will enable their staff to make use of the resources these projects will provide. Where training is on a multi-agency basis, costs should be shared appropriately.

Other Staff

8.8 Telephonists and receptionists in the different agencies involved in services for children should be given clear instructions on what to do if contacted by anyone wishing to report suspected child abuse.

PART NINE: CASE REVIEWS

Introduction

9.1 A Case Review by management in each involved agency should be instigated in all cases that involve the death of, or serious harm to a child where child abuse is confirmed or suspected. These cases cause distress within the family, create distress and anxiety among the staff of the agencies, and arouse public concern. Agencies need to respond quickly and positively to ensure that their services are maintained and are not undermined by the incident, that public concern is allayed and media comment is answered in a positive manner. The timely production of a well conducted case review report with clear conclusions, and where necessary positive recommendations for action should in most cases enable agencies to ensure that all necessary lessons are learned and public concern satisfied.

9.2 The detailed handling of a case review will depend on the circumstances of the case and the different organisational structures of the individual agencies. The following paragraphs cover the general principles and the review process in the context of inter-agency co-operation. They do not address the arrangements within individual agencies.

Inter-agency co-operation

9.3 Close co-operation between agencies through the ACPC is important as case reviews are set in hand and progress. A complete picture of the events can only be built up in collaboration with other agencies involved. The most effective case review report will be one that has been conducted in the light of guidance from the ACPC and within the local procedures for collaboration. If criminal investigations are proceeding and prosecution is being considered it will be particularly important for agencies to be aware of the action police or the prosecuting authority are undertaking.

9.4 The ACPC should provide the focus for ensuring: co-operative and co-ordinated action from the outset; that all local agencies that have been, or could have been, involved with the child and family are immediately informed of action planned; that the findings of the Case Reviews are brought together to form an overall picture of service provision in the case and advice attached on the need for any future action. The ACPC should agree in advance the most suitable way of undertaking these tasks. It may be helpful either to establish a permanent Sub-Committee to consider case reviews or to agree the framework under which a Sub-Committee can be set up quickly if and when the need arises. It will be important to inform the Chairman of the ACPC of the arrangements in a particular case including the time table for completion of the exercise.

9.5 A picture of what happened should be built up through case reviews within each of the agencies involved having regard to the differing management structures within each agency. In each agency, the senior officer will need to designate someone to undertake the review, to ensure that progress is not impeded and to arrange, if necessary, appropriate cover for the normal duties of the person conducting the review. The Health Authority and Social Services Committees and parent authorities of other agencies as appropriate will need to be kept informed in accordance with locally agreed procedures.

9.6 Notwithstanding police enquiries the momentum of the individual case reviews should be maintained and the need for action considered by the ACPC. The case reviews should be completed within two or three weeks and the recommendations for future action presented to the appropriate authorities by the ACPC within seven working days of all relevant individual reports being provided to them. This should ensure that agencies have clear indications of the situation leading up to the case – as well as the recommendations for future action – within one month of the case arising.

General principles

9.7 The following underlying principles are identified as important. Their degree of relevance will depend upon the nature of the case and type of review:

a. *Urgency*: Agencies should take action immediately and follow this through as quickly as possible.
b. *Impartiality*: Those conducting the review should not have been directly concerned with the child or family.
c. *Thoroughness*: All important factors should be considered and there should be an opportunity for all those involved to contribute.
d. *Openness*: There should be no suspicion of concealment. This means quick and clear communication with elected members and the public.
e. *Confidentiality*: Due regard must be paid to the balance of individuals' rights and the public interest.
f. *Co-operation*: The local ACPC should provide a framework to ensure close co-operation between all the agencies involved.
g. *Resolution*: Action should be taken to implement any recommendations that may arise and are accepted by the agencies concerned.

Purpose of review

9.8 The overall purpose of the review should be to secure the best possible quality of services to children and their families. The specific action should have five main objectives:

a. To establish facts.
b. To assess whether decisions and actions taken in the case were reasonable and responsible.
c. To check whether established procedures were followed.
d. To consider whether the services provided matched the needs of the case bearing in mind the resources available.
e. To recommend any appropriate action in the light of the review's findings.

The review process

9.9 *Fact Finding*: The initial task of the review will be to verify the facts; it is vital therefore that records relating to the case are immediately secured against interference or loss. It will be necessary to construct a diary of events to obtain a complete picture of the case. Individual agencies will need, in the context of their own review, to assess this from their own service perspective. The establishment of a comprehensive diary reflecting the involvement of all agencies will require inter-agency co-operation.

9.10 *Staff Interests*: Managers will need to ensure that staff directly involved in the case are informed of the purpose of the review and the way that it will be conducted. This will help to reduce anxiety and, with management support, enable staff to continue providing a service to their other clients. Trade unions and professional associations and staff not directly involved in the case should also be kept informed of progress and it should be made clear in all these discussions that the review is separate from, even if it leads to, any action that may be necessary under established disciplinary procedures.

9.11 *Public and Media Interests*: It is inevitable that some cases will attract strong public and media interest. Agencies should have a clear policy on, and appoint persons to act as a point of contact with, the media. The importance of keeping the media and public informed should be recognised and there should be close co-operation between agencies on the release of statements. Agencies will need to consult their legal advisers and the police to ensure that nothing is made public in contempt of court or in any way prejudicial to any civil or criminal proceedings.

Information for DHSS and Welsh Office

9.12 Local Authorities are required to inform DHSS and Welsh Office as appropriate, when a child in care in their area dies or is seriously harmed and child abuse is suspected. As indicated at paragraph 9.1 above, Authorities in England and Wales should conduct an internal management case review in any situation in which a child has suffered death or serious injury. When a case review has been undertaken, a copy of the ACPC Report should be provided to DHSS or Welsh Office, and the Departments should be notified of any action that Authorities intend to commission before a management review is undertaken. The information will provide notice of cases which may arouse acute public concern, allow the Departments to keep the guidance in this paper under review and identify implications for child abuse policy generally. In addition, the Departments will:

a. determine whether any particular comment is needed from the centre on matters of professional or other practice in relation to the particular case;
b. where necessary examined the progress made in implementing a management review's recommendations in the context of subsequent pre-planned survey or investigation round.

9.13 The management review need not exclude the conduct of any other action that the Authority or Authorities concerned consider to be necessary or appropriate – for example to provide for an independent evaluation (as opposed to local independent inquiry) covering matters of professional practice in a given case. The channel for the provision of information in these matters should continue to be either from the local authority social services departments to the regional office of the DHSS Social Service Inspectorate, or from Health Authorities to DHSS Regional Liaison Division. In Wales, information from Social Services Departments should be relayed to the Social Work Services Division – and from Health Authorities to HSSP1 Division – of the Welsh Office.

The Police

9.14 The police on behalf of the coroner, will conduct an investigation into the cause of the death of a child and into whether anybody is criminally responsible for it. Witnesses will be interviewed and written statements obtained. Where the police consider that there is evidence against a person of an offence of homicide they may charge that person and must refer the case to the Crown Prosecution Service (CPS). Thereafter the conduct of the case is undertaken by the CPS who will decide whether the evidence is sufficient for proceedings for homicide and, if so, will arrange for the case to be brought to trial. The Coroner's Inquest will be adjourned pending the outcome of the prosecution. In other cases involving harm to a child the police may conduct an investigation and the CPS may prosecute any person who they consider has committed a criminal offence in respect of the child.

Subsequent action

9.15 The aim of the case review should be to ensure that any lessons from the events under review are acted upon promptly and effectively. Problems of inter-agency concern should be considered by the ACPC who will need to monitor the implementation of agreed changes, details of which should be published. In their overview report to the agencies on the case reviews, the ACPC should indicate whether there are aspects of the case which seem to justify further inquiry. It will then be for the agencies individually or jointly to consider what form an inquiry will take.

Appendix 1

Related Guidance

Diagnosis of Child Sexual Abuse Guidance for Doctors: Standing Medical Advisory Committee's report published simultaneously with Working Together.

Child Protection: Guidance for Senior Nurses, Health Visitors and Midwives: Standing Nursing and Midwifery Advisory Committee report published simultaneously with Working Together.

Practice Guide to Social Workers on Assessment: DHSS report to be published October 1988.

Home Office Circular of 1988 The Investigation of Child Sex Abuse: issued simultaneously with Working Together.

Department of Education and Science Circular on Child Abuse: issued simultaneously with Working Together.

Code of Practice – Access to Children in Care: DHSS published in 1983.

The Report of The Inquiry Into Child Abuse in Cleveland 1987: HMSO published July 1988.

The Force Response to Child Abuse Within the Family – The Principles and Code of Practice: Metropolitan Police published 1987.

Ad Hoc Inquiries in Local Government: SOLACE published 1988.

Report of the Working Group on Publicity for the Prevention of Child abuse: Home Office Standing Conference on Crime Prevention: published 1987.

Metropolitan Police and Bexley Social Services Child Sexual Abuse Investigative Experiment Final Report: Home Office published 1987.

The Legal Framework

This appendix sets out the content of the main legislative provisions discussed in the guide; staff should consult their legal advisers on the application of these provisions to individual cases.

LOCAL AUTHORITIES

Duty to Investigate

The duty of the local authority to investigate information received suggesting that a child may need protection is described in section 2 of the Children and Young Persons Act 1969:

'(1) If a local authority receives information suggesting that there are grounds for bringing care proceedings in respect of a child or young person who resides or is found in their area, it shall be the duty of the authority to cause inquiries to be made into the case unless they are satisfied that such inquiries are unnecessary.'

and is implicit in the Child Care Act 1980, section 2(1):

'Where it appears to a local authority with respect to a child in their area appearing to them to be under the age of seventeen:

a. that he has neither parent nor guardian or has been and remains abandoned by his parents or guardian or is lost; or
b. that his parents or guardian are, for the time being or permanently, prevented by reason of mental and bodily disease or infirmity or other incapacity of any other circumstances from providing for his proper accommodation, maintenance and upbringing; and
c. in either case, that the intervention of the local authority under this section is necessary in the interests of the welfare of the child,

it shall be the duty of the local authority to receive the child into their care under this section.'

Prevention

The general duty of the local authority to promote the welfare of children and to take preventive action is described in section 1(1) of the Child Care Act 1980 as follows:

'It shall be the duty of every local authority to make available such advice, guidance and assistance as may promote the welfare of children by diminishing the need to receive children into or keep them in care under this Act or to bring children before a juvenile court; and any provision made by a local authority under this sub-section may, if the local authority think fit, include provision for giving assistance in kind or, in exceptional circumstances, in cash.'

Reception into Care – Voluntary Care

The grounds for receiving children into voluntary care are described in section 2(1) of the Child Care Act 1980 as follows:

'Where it appears to a local authority with respect to a child in their area appearing to them to be under the age of 17:

a. that he has neither parent or guardian or has been and remains abandoned by his parents or guardian or is lost; or
b. that his parents or guardian are, for the time being or permanently, prevented by reason of mental and bodily disease or infirmity or other incapacity or any other circumstances from providing for his proper accommodation, maintenance and upbringing; and
c. in either case, that the intervention of the local authority under this section is necessary in the interests of the welfare of the child,

it shall be the duty of the local authority to receive the child into their care under this section.'

Care Proceedings

The grounds, some of which are specifically related to child abuse, which have to be satisfied in care proceedings before a court can make a care order under section 1 of the Children and Young Persons Act 1969 (as amended) are set out in section 1(2) as follows:

'(2) If the court before which a child or young person is brought under this section is of opinion that any of the following conditions is satisfied with respect to him, that is to say:

a. his proper development is being avoidably prevented or neglected or his health is being avoidably impaired or neglected or he is being ill treated; or
b. it is probable that the condition set out in the preceding paragraph will be satisfied in his case, having regard to the fact that the court or another court has found that that condition is or was satisfied in the case of another child or young person who is or was a member of the household to which he belongs; or
bb. it is probable that the condition set out in paragraph (a) of this sub section will be satisfied in his case, having regard to the fact that a

person who has been convicted of an offence mentioned in Schedule 1 to the Act of 1933, including a person convicted of such an offence on whose conviction for the offence an order was made under Part I of the Powers of Criminal Courts Act 1973 placing him on probation or discharging him absolutely or conditionally is, or may become, a member of the same household as the child or young person;

c. he is exposed to moral danger; or
d. he is beyond the control of his parent or guardian; or
e. he is of compulsory school age within the meaning of the Education Act 1944 and is not receiving efficient full-time education suitable to his age, ability and aptitude and to any special educational needs he may have; or
f. he is guilty of an offence, excluding homicide;

and also that he is in need of care or control which he is unlikely to receive unless the court makes an order under this section in respect of him, then, subject to the following provisions of this section and sections 2 and 3 of this Act, the court may if it thinks fit make such an order.'

Emergency Situations

Under section 28(1) of the Children and Young Persons Act 1969 (the 1969 Act) a child or young person may be removed to a place of safety for not more than 28 days on application by any person to a Justice. The section provides:

'If, upon application to a Justice by any person for authority to detain a child or young person and take him to a place of safety, the Justice is satisfied that the applicant has reasonable cause to believe that:

a. Any of the conditions set out in section 1(2)(a) to (e) of this Act is satisfied in respect of the child or young person; or
b. an appropriate court would find the conditions set out in section 1(2)(b) of this Act satisfied in respect of him; or
c. the child or young person is about to leave the United Kingdom in contravention of section 25 of the Act of 1933 (which regulates the sending abroad of juvenile entertainers);

the Justice may grant the application; and the child or young person in respect of whom an authorisation is issued under this sub-section may be detained in a place of safety by virtue of the authorisation for 28 days beginning with the date of authorisation, or such shorter period beginning with that date as may be specified in the authorisation.'

The conditions mentioned in paragraphs (a) and (b) are those which may be grounds for seeking a care order, and are set out under Care Proceedings in this Annex.

Section 28(2) of the 1969 Act authorises a constable to detain a child or young person without application to a Justice for not more than 8 days on similar grounds except the conditions set out in section 1(2)(e) (or if he is satisfied that an offence is being committed under section 10(1) of the Children and Young Persons Act, 1933 which penalises a vagrant for taking a juvenile from place to place).

Section 28(3) requires notification of detention to the child and his parents or guardian as soon as practicable after detention.

Under **section 40 of the Children and Young Persons Act 1933** a warrant to search for or remove a child or young person may be obtained:

'(1) If it appears to a Justice of the Peace on information on oath laid by any persons who, in the opinion of the Justice is acting in the interests of a child or young person, that there is reasonable cause to suspect:

a. that the child or young person has been or is being assaulted, ill-treated, or neglected in any place within the jurisdiction of the Justice, in a manner likely to cause him unnecessary suffering, or injury to health; or

b. that any offence mentioned in the First Schedule to this Act has been or is being committed in respect of the child or young person;

the Justice may issue a warrant authorising any constable named therein to search for the child or young person, and, if it is found that he has been or is being assaulted, ill-treated, or neglected in manner aforesaid, or that any such offence as aforesaid has been or is being committed in respect of him, to take him to a place of safety, or authorising any constable to remove him with or without search to a place of safety, and a child or young person taken to a place of safety in pursuance of such a warrant may be detained there until he can be brought before a juvenile court.

(2) A Justice issuing a warrant under this section may by the same warrant cause any person accused of any offence in respect of the child or young person to be apprehended and brought before a court of summary jurisdiction, and proceedings to be taken against him according to law.

(3) Any constable authorised by warrant under this section to search for any child or young person, or to remove any child or young person with or without search, may enter (if need be by force) any house, building, or other place specified in the warrant, and may remove him therefrom.

(4) Every warrant issued under this section shall be addressed to and executed by a constable, who shall be accompanied by the person laying the information, if that person so desires, unless the Justice by whom the warrant is issued otherwise directs, and may also, if the Justice by whom the warrant is issued so directs, be accompanied by a duly qualified medical practitioner.

(5) It shall not be necessary in any information or warrant under this Section to name the child or young person.'

See also section 23 of the Children and Young Persons Act 1963 which applies to section 40 detentions in a place of safety.

Section 14 of the Armed Forces Act 1981 (as amended by the 1986 Act) provides for the temporary removal to and detention in a place of safety abroad of children of service families in need of care or control.

'(1) This section applies to a child who:

a. forms part of the family of a person subject to service law serving in a country or territory outside the United Kingdom or of a civilian in a corresponding position;
b. resides outside the United Kingdom with that family or another such family; and
c. is under seventeen years of age and unmarried.

(2) This section also applies to a child who is staying (for however short a time) with a family other than the family to which he belongs but otherwise satisfies the conditions specified in sub-section (1) above and so applies to him as if he resided with that family.

(3) If an officer having jurisdiction in relation to a child to whom this section applies thinks fit, he may, on being satisfied on one or more of the grounds specified in sub-section (4) below that the child is in need of care and control, order the child to be removed to and detained in a place of safety.

(4) The grounds which justify the making of such an order in relation to a child to whom this section applies are:

a. that his proper development is being avoidably prevented or neglected or his health is being avoidably impaired or neglected or he is being or is likely to be ill-treated;
b. that he is exposed to moral danger;
c. that he is beyond the control of his parent or guardian or, in a case where the child resides for the time being with the family of another person, of that person.

(4A) A place of safety in which a child is required to be detained under this section may be situated either in the country or territory where the child resides or elsewhere (including in the United Kingdom); and an officer having jurisdiction in relation to a child detained in a place of safety outside the United Kingdom may make an order (including an order involving the return of the child to the United Kingdom) modifying the order by which the child is detained so as to require the child to be removed to and detained in another place of safety.

(5) The officers having jurisdiction in relation to a child to whom this section applies or a child detained in a place of safety are:

a. the commanding officer of the person to whose family the child belongs;
b. the commanding officer of the person with whose family the child resides or, as the case may be, was residing when he was removed to a place of safety.'

Equivalent provisions apply to the Air Force and Navy under the Air Force Act 1955 and the Naval Discipline Act 1957 (both as amended).

Supervision orders

Sections 11–19 of the Children and Young Persons Act 1969 set out provisions relating to supervision orders:

Section 11 states

'Any provision of this Act authorising a court to make a supervision order in respect of any person shall be construed as authorising the court to make an order placing him under the supervision of a local authority designated by the order or of a probation officer: and in this Act "supervised person" shall be construed accordingly and "supervised person" and "supervisor", in relation to a supervision order, mean respectively the person placed or to be placed under supervision by the order and the person under whose supervision he is placed or to be placed by order.'

The power to include requirements in supervision orders is set out in Section 12:

'(1) A supervision order may require the supervised person to reside with an individual named in the order who agrees to the requirement, but a requirement imposed by a supervision order in pursuance of this sub-section shall be subject to any such requirement of the order as is authorised by the following provisions of this section.

(2) Subject to section 19(12) of this Act, a supervision order may require the supervised person to comply with any directions given from time to time by the supervisor and requiring him to do all or any of the following things:

a. to live at a place or places specified in the directions for a period or periods so specified;
b. to present himself to a person or persons specified in the directions at a place or places and on a day or days so specified;
c. to participate in activities specified in the directions on a day or days so specified;

but it shall be for the supervisor to decide whether and to what extent he exercises any power to give directions conferred on him by virtue of the preceding provisions of this sub-section and to decide the form of any directions; and a requirement imposed by a supervision order in pursuance of this sub-section shall be subject to any such requirement of the order as is authorised by sub-section (4) of this section.'

[requirements sub-sections (3)–(5) not quoted]

Section 14 sets out the duties of a supervisor:

'While a supervision order is in force it shall be the duty of the supervisor to advise, assist and befriend the supervised person.'

Section 15 allows for the variation and discharge of a supervision order and the substitution of a care order:

'(1) If while a supervision order is in force in respect of a supervised person who has not attained the age of eighteen it appears to a juvenile court, on the application of the supervisor or the supervised person, that it is appropriate to make an order under this sub-section, the court may make an order discharging the supervision order or varying it by:

a. cancelling any requirement included in it in pursuance of section 12 or section 18(2)(b) of this Act; or
b. inserting in it (either in addition to or in substitution for any of its provisions) any provision which could have been included in the order if the court had then had power to make it and were exercising the power, and may on discharging the supervision order make a care order (other than an interim order) in respect of the supervised person.'

Care Orders

Section 1(2) of the Children and Young Persons Act 1969 sets out the grounds which need to be satisfied before a court will grant a care order. This section is quoted above under care proceedings. Section 1(3) of the same Act sets out the type of order which the court may make under section 1:

'a. an order requiring his parent or guardian to enter into a recognisance to take proper care of him and exercise proper control over him; or
b. a supervision order; or
c. a care order (other than an interim order); or
d. a hospital order within the meaning of Part III of the Mental Health Act 1983; or
e. a guardianship order within the meaning of that Act.'

Section 10 of the Child Care Act 1980 sets out the powers and duties of local authorities with respect to children committed to their care:

'(1) It shall be the duty of a local authority to whose care a child is committed by a care order or by a warrant under section 23(1) of the Children and Young Persons Act 1969 (which relates to remands in the care of local authorities) to receive the child into their care and, notwithstanding any claim by his parent or guardian, to keep him in their care while the order or warrant is in force.

(2) A local authority shall, subject to the following provisions of this section, have the same powers and duties with respect to a person in their care by virtue of a care order or such a warrant as his parent or guardian would have apart from the order or warrant and may (without prejudice to the foregoing provisions of this sub-section but subject to regulations made in pursuance of section 39 of this Act) restrict his liberty to such extent as the authority consider appropriate.

(3) A local authority shall not cause a child in their care by virtue of a care order to be brought up in any religious creed other than that in which he would have been brought up apart from the order.

(4) It shall be the duty of a local authority to comply with any provision included in an interim order in pursuance of section 22(2) of the Children and Young Persons Act 1969 and, in the case of a person in their care by virtue of section 23 of that Act, to permit him to be removed from their care in due course of law.'

Responsibility of Local Authority for Children in Care

In discharging its responsibilities for children in care, whether they have been received or voluntarily placed into care, or committed into care by a court order, the local authority must act in accordance with its duty under section 18(1) of the Child Care Act 1980, which sets out the so-called 'welfare principle'. That sub-section states:

'In reaching any decision relating to a child in their care, a local authority shall give first consideration to the need to safeguard and promote the welfare of the child throughout his childhood; and shall so far as practicable ascertain the wishes and feelings of the child regarding the decision and give due consideration to them, having regard to his age and understanding.'

CO-OPERATION OF LOCAL AND HEALTH AUTHORITIES

National Health Service Act 1977

Co-operation and Assistance

Section 22 of the 1977 Act requires that in exercising their respective functions health authorities and local authorities shall co-operate with one another in order to secure and advance the health and welfare of the people of England and Wales.

SCHEDULE 8

Local Social Services Authorities

Care of Mothers and Young Children

1(1) A local social services authority may, with the Secretary of State's approval, and to such extent as he may direct shall, make arrangements for the care of expectant and nursing mothers and of children who have not attained the age of 5 years and are not attending primary schools maintained by a local education authority.

Prevention, Care and After-care

2(1) A local social services authority may, with the Secretary of State's approval, and to such extent as he may direct shall, make arrangements for the purpose of the prevention of illness and for the care of persons suffering from illness and for the after-care of persons who have been so suffering and in particular for:

a. the provision, equipment and maintenance of residential accommodation for the care of persons with a view to preventing them from becoming ill, the care of persons suffering from illness and the after-care of persons who have been so suffering;
b. the provision, for persons whose care is undertaken with a view to preventing them from becoming ill, persons suffering from illness and persons who have been so suffering, of centres or other facilities for training them or keeping them suitably occupied and the equipment and maintenance of such centres;
c. the provision, for the benefit of such persons as are mentioned in paragraph (b) above, of ancillary or supplemental services; and
d. as regards persons suffering from mental disorder within the meaning of the Mental Health Act 1959, the appointment of officers to act as mental welfare officers under that Act and, in the case of such persons so suffering as are received into guardianship under Part IV of that Act (whether the guardianship of the local social services authority or of other persons), the exercise of the functions of the authority in respect of them.

Such an authority shall neither have the power nor be subject to a duty to make under this paragraph arrangements to provide facilities for any of the purposes mentioned in section 15(1) of the Disabled Persons (Employment) Act 1944.

(2) No arrangements under this paragraph shall provide for the payment of money to persons for whose benefit they are made except:

a. in so far as they may provide for the remuneration of such persons engaged in suitable work in accordance with the arrangements; or
b. to persons who:

   i. are, or have been, suffering from mental disorder within the meaning of [the Mental Health Act 1983];
   ii. are under the age of 16 years; and
   iii. are resident in accommodation provided under the arrangements, of such amounts as the local social services authority think fit in respect of their occasional personal expenses where it appears to that authority that no such payment would otherwise be made.

(3) The Secretary of State may make regulations as to the conduct of premises in which, in pursuance of arrangements made under this paragraph, are provided for persons whose care is undertaken with a view to preventing them from becoming sufferers from mental disorder within the meaning of [that Act of 1983] or who are, or have been, so suffering, residential accommodation or facilities for training them or keeping them suitably occupied.

(4) Any such regulations may in particular confer on the Secretary of State's officers so authorised such powers of inspection as may be prescribed by the regulations.

Home help and laundry facilities

3(1) It is the duty of every local social services authority to provide on such a scale as is adequate for the needs of their area, or to arrange for the provision on such a scale as is so adequate, of home help for households where such help is required owing to the presence of:

a. a person who is suffering from illness, lying-in, an expectant mother, aged, handicapped as a result of having suffered from illness or by congenital deformity; or

b. a child who has not attained the age which, for the purposes of the Education Act 1944 is, in his case, the upper limit of the compulsory school age;

and every such authority has power to provide or arrange for the provision of laundry facilities for households for which home help is being, or can be, provided under this sub-paragraph.

Armed Services Arrangements for Child Abuse

1. This Appendix offers guidance to cover service families, for inclusion in local procedural handbooks.

Forces based in England and Wales

2. The Service Authorities seek to co-operate with statutory agencies and to support service families where child abuse occurs. The information they hold on any family can help in the assessment and review of child abuse cases. Procedures exist in all the services for the registration and monitoring of the protection of children and the usual rules of confidentiality are observed. In working together the services authorities and the local authority social services department need to keep in mind that legislation places the primary responsibility for the care and protection of children on the local authority.

Army

3. The welfare of army families whose children are considered to be at risk by a social services department is the responsibility of the Army Families Housing and Welfare Service (FHWS). Social services departments should liaise with one of the 55 FHWS Commandants (managers) who between them provide cover for the whole of the UK. Contact telephone numbers are given at the end of this Appendix.

Royal Navy and Royal Marines

4. The Navy Personnel and Families Service (NPFS) provides qualified social workers in 3 area teams, each headed by an area officer. Their telephone numbers are given at the end of this Appendix.

Royal Air Force

5. The Royal Air Force does not have an independent welfare organisation. Social work is managed as a normal function of command and co-ordinated by each Station's Personnel Officer; the Officer Commanding Personnel Management Squadron (OCPMS). Whenever a child abuse investigation concerns the child of a serving member of the RAF, the social services department should notify the parents' unit, or if this is not known, the nearest RAF unit by contacting the Officer Commanding Personnel Management Squadron. Every RAF unit has an officer appointed to this duty and he will be familiar with child abuse procedures.

Service Families going or returning from overseas

6. The Soldiers', Sailors' and Airmen's Families Association (SSAFA) provides, at the request of the Ministry of Defence, a qualified social work and health visiting service for families of all services on overseas stations.

7. Where there is a child protection plan in this country for a child in a service family who are to move overseas, the social services department concerned should notify SSAFA in writing with full documentation, case summary, case conference notes, etc. This information is forwarded to the relevant SSAFA social worker overseas in order that:

a. the case may be entered on the overseas British Forces Child Protection Register;
b. the practitioners at the overseas base can be alerted and a case conference arranged; and
c. appropriate support and supervision are provided to the family.

8. Similarly, when a service family with a child in need of protection returns to the UK, it is SSAFA's responsibility to contact the social services department in whose area they will be living and ensure that full documentation is provided to assist in the management of the case. Where there is a statutory involvement (eg Supervision Order), SSAFA will provide regular reports to the local authority concerned.

Emergency Action regarding Service Families Abroad   Armed Forces Act 1981
(as amended by Armed Forces Act 1966)
See Appendix 1

9. When it appears that a child is in urgent need of care or control an officer having jurisdiction in relation to the child may order the child to be removed to and detained in a place of safety. If the officer makes an order to transfer the child to the United Kingdom so that care of the child can become the responsibility of the relevant local authority all necessary action will be arranged and agreed before hand between the responsible agencies concerned.

UK Armed Services: Contact Points

10. A. Army

Controller FHWS, HQ UKLF	Salisbury 0722-336222 (ask for) Ext Old Sarum 221/126/127
Principal Commandants FHWS	North-Eastern District (York) 0904-59811 Ext 2541
	North-West District (Preston) 0772-716543 Ext 473
	Western District (Shrewsbury) 0743-52234 Ext 202
	Eastern District (Colchester) 0206-575121 Ext 2166/2463
	South-West District (Bulford Camp) 09803-3371 Ext 4466/4865
	London District (Horseguards SW1) 01-930-4466 Ext 2246
	Scotland (Edinburgh) 031-336-1761 Ext 6371
	Wales (Brecon) 0874-3111 Ext 305

B. Royal Navy

	Western Area (Plymouth) 0752-58611 Ext 5041/2
	Eastern Area (Portsmouth) 0705-820932 Ext 23533/4
	Northern Area (Inverkiething) 0383/41647 or 410111

C. SSAFA

Assistant Director, SSAFA Nursing and Social Work Service	Salisbury 0722-26345

Armed Services: Contact Points (for Northern Ireland)

A. Army

Principal Commandant F H W S   Northern Ireland (Lisburn)
08462-5111 Ext 42734

B. Royal Navy

No NI entry necessary. NI interests covered by Northern Area.

C. SSAFA   Northern Ireland (Lisburn)
08462-89008

USAF

11. Each local authority with an American base in their area should have established liaison arrangements with the Base Commander and relevant staff. British child protection and care legislation should be set out and requirements made clear to the USAF authorities so that local authorities can ensure that they are able to fulfill their statutory duties.

Child Protection Register

This Appendix lists the data to be held on the Register.

Part I: Identification

1. Child's full name, other names known to be used, home address, sex, date and place of birth.

2. Location (if not at home).

3. Legal status of child when first placed on the register (register to be amended on every change in legal status).

4. Full names (including maiden names), known other names used and addresses of parents or others caring for the child and the name and address of any other adult members of, or regular visitors to the household, together with information on their relationship to the child.

5. Details of any relevant offences of any person mentioned at 4 above.

6. Full names, dates of birth and sex of other children in the household, care status where appropriate and whether they are also on the Child Protection Register.

Part II: Nature of Abuse

7. Date of first referral to statutory agency.

8. Indication of categories of abuse in the case. (Use categories as set out in DHSS statistical return. See Part Five).

Part III: Key worker and Core Group

9. Name of key worker and telephone number.

10. Other agencies providing services to the child and family, including identification of core group.

11. GP's name, address and telephone number.

12. HV's name, address and telephone number.

13. Child's school, play group, nursery or child minder, if any; including name of teacher, etc and telephone number.

14. Referral, source of original request for investigation, and date.

15. Note of area to which a child has moved and office to which case records transferred.

16. Date of plan (ie registration date).

17. Date when parents or carers told of plan. If they have not been told of registration reason for this.

18. Programme of review (ie timing, method etc).

19. Date of reviews.

20. Date when inter-agency reviewing ended (ie deregistration) or date when child moved from area, new address and arrangements made for handover to agencies in new area eg conferences held, records transferred etc.

All staff involved with the child and family should notify changes in this information to the key worker so that the register may be kept up to date.

Appendix 5

Area Child Protection Committees (ACPCs)

1. The ACPC must concern itself with the full range of services provided by the agencies described in Parts Two to Four of the guide. It is recommended that formal membership should include senior officers of the following main services:

a. **Social service agencies**

   i. Local authority social services department

   ii. National Society for the Prevention of Cruelty to Children (NSPCC)

b. **Health Authority**

   i. Health Service Management

   ii. Medical and Psychiatric Services

   iii. Nursing

c. **Family Practitioner Services**

   i. FPC

   ii. GP

d. **Education Services**

   i. Education authority

   ii. Teachers

e. **Police**

f. **Probation Service**

g. **Armed services** – where appropriate and particularly if there is a major service base in the area.

2. In addition, it will be important for the Committee to establish links with:

i.   Local authority housing departments;

ii. General Dental Practitioner Services;

iii. Local Social Security Offices;

iv. Voluntary agencies providing relevant services;

v. Organisations representing religious and cultural interests.

Appendix 6

Content and Format of Local Procedural Handbooks

1. The Guide recommends that the structure and content of local procedural handbooks concerned with the handling of inter-agency issues should be standardised. The recommended standard content is set out below.

Section I: Law and Definitions

a. The legal framework for work to protect children from harm at the hands of their parents.
b. Definitions of child abuse and the criteria for placing a child's name on the child protection register.

Section II: Who is involved

a. The roles of statutory agencies and how child abuse work fits into their more general areas of work and the child welfare responsibilities of authorities – particularly to children in care.
b. The contribution of other agencies and independent practitioners.

Section III: Recognition and Investigation

a. How members of the public and staff locally should refer any concern they have about individual children.
b. The central roles of local authority social services departments, (or the NSPCC) and the police in investigating suspected cases.
c. The steps that the social services department (or the NSPCC) and the police will take to investigate cases, including holding strategy discussions or meetings and the use of specialist assessment teams.
d. The contributions from other agencies, including the role of medical and health staff in seeking to establish the significance of injuries or other evidence of possible abuse.

Section IV: Assessment and Planning

a. How staff in other agencies may be involved in inter-agency discussions aimed at developing an agreed plan of action.
b. To describe the role of the key worker who will have case responsibility.
c. How parents should be involved in developing a plan of action.

Section V: Implementation and Review

a. The purpose of the child protection register.
b. The process of reviewing progress to ensure that the plans and objectives are being achieved.
c. The procedure for removing a child's name from the register.

Section VI: Local Agency Procedures

a. Agreed procedures to be followed by individual agencies for their own staff.
b. Procedures when a registered child moves into or out of an area.
c. Advice on special circumstances, for example children of service families. (See Appendix 3).

2. **The recommended format of handbooks** is set out below.

a. A loose-leaf form, to aid regular review and revision of the material.
b. Full indexes should be provided.
c. Concisely worded, short paragraphs.
d. Good typography to highlight important points.

Child Abuse Management Information

The recommended contents of information that should be provided to the ACPC is set out below.

I. Information from the child protection register

a. Current cases:
To illustrate the characteristics of the children currently on the register eg, age/sex, type of abuse etc.
b. Sources of original referrals for investigation of cases currently on the register.
c. Cases removed from the register:
The number and types of cases for which formalised inter-agency collaboration has ceased, ie cases taken off the register or cases transferred to another area.

II. Information from the record on enquiries to the register

a. Number and source (ie agency) of enquiries about children on the register.
b. Number and source (ie agency) of enquiries about children not on the register.

III. Records related to the use of statutory powers on an emergency basis

a. Number of applications for place of safety orders with reason for the application.
b. Number granted.
c. Eventual child care status.

IV. Information from other records

The level of child abuse work eg number, frequency and average duration of case conferences held.

Child Abuse Annual Report

The outline format recommended for the report is set out below.

Section I: Prevention

To describe the action taken to identify vulnerable children and families and provide help and support.

Section II: Protection

To describe the action taken:

a. to ensure that members of the public and practitioners in all agencies are aware how they can report any concern they have for individual children.
b. to protect individual children, the number of cases investigated, information about the plans of action and number of cases concluded.
c. to include information on trends over time, different types of abuse, etc. Information (in anonymous terms) to compile this element of the report would be drawn from the management information report compiled (see Appendix 7).
d. on the outcome of any case review or inquiry into serious cases of abuse.

Section III: Policy and Procedures

To describe relevant agency or inter-agency policy and procedural changes related to child abuse made during the year and to set out forward plans for the year ahead.

Section IV: Training

To describe action taken by individual agencies and collectively to:

a. reinforce the awareness of staff over the indicators of child abuse;
b. improve knowledge and skills of practitioners in handling of child abuse cases.

Appendix 9

Child Abuse Reviews

Glossary of Terms

ACPC:	Area Child Protection Committee
Agency:	this term covers both public bodies and voluntary organisations.
Authority:	a public body which has statutory powers or duties, or both.
Case Review (by Management):	a review of the way in which services to the child and family had been provided; an integral part of the agency's function to monitor its standards.
Inquiry:	an inquiry conducted after case reviews by agencies when a need for a second level of investigation has been identified.
Management:	in the context of this paper the term must be interpreted broadly to reflect the different organisational structures within agencies responsible for service provision, for instance:
Social Services Departments:	It is anticipated that the Director of Social Services would nominate a senior officer to undertake the case review.
Health Authorities:	District General Manager to co-ordinate a review of services and to report to the Regional Health Authority or Welsh Office as necessary and to arrange co-operation with case reviews.

Palindromic numbers.
as a palindrome

Hospital Medical Services:	Each consultant head of a clinical team would need to study his team's involvement with the child and family and the services they had provided, and to arrange co-operation with reviews.
Community Medical Services:	The senior community physician should study his team's involvement with the child and family and the services they had provided and co-operate with case reviews.
Nursing Services:	Each separate unit within the nursing management would need to review its own services; to co-ordinate this the District Nursing Officer should nominate a senior nurse who is not in immediate managerial relationship with the member of staff concerned with the case. The nominated person should arrange co-operation with any case review.
General Medical:	The GP should consider his involvement with the individual patients within the family – and be prepared, with help from professional colleagues and/or the local Medical Committee, to produce sufficient information to allow the ACPC to consider fully the services provided to the child and family.

Printed in the United Kingdom for HMSO.
Dd.0293593, 2/91, C20, 3390/3, 5673, 133708.